ROMANS 1

ANCIENT TEXTS & MORMON STUDIES

NUMBER 1

John W. Welch, Series Editor
John A. Tvedtnes, Associate Series Editor

This series presents a wide-ranging collection of important ancient texts that are of interest to Latter-day Saints. Each volume includes the ancient text, a readable translation, technical notes, and general commentary. These materials tell what is known about the historical origins and ancient purposes of the text and show its main points of value to modern religious readers.

ROMANS 1
NOTES AND REFLECTIONS

JAMES E. FAULCONER

FOUNDATION FOR ANCIENT RESEARCH AND MORMON STUDIES
AT BRIGHAM YOUNG UNIVERSITY
PROVO, UTAH

James E. Faulconer earned a Ph.D. in Philosophy from Pennsylvania State University. He currently serves as Dean of General Education and Honors and is Professor of Philosophy at Brigham Young University.

Cover design by Bjorn W. Pendleton

The Foundation for Ancient Research and Mormon Studies (FARMS)
at Brigham Young University
P.O. Box 7113
University Station
Provo, Utah 84602

Library of Congress Cataloging-in-Publication Data

Faulconer, James E.
   Romans 1 : notes and reflections/James E. Faulconer.
     p. cm. — (Ancient texts and Mormon studies, ISSN 1526-4386 ; no. 1)
   Includes bibliographical references and indexes.
   ISBN 0-934893-44-6 (pbk. : alk. paper)
   1. Bible. N.T. Romans—Commentaries. 2. Church of Jesus Christ of Latter-Day Saints—Doctrines. I. Title. II. Series.

   BS2665.3 .F38 1999
   227'.1077—dc21   99-049201

CONTENTS

FARMS Publications

Teachings of the Book of Mormon

The Geography of Book of Mormon Events: A Source Book

The Book of Mormon Text Reformatted according to Parallelistic Patterns

Eldin Ricks's Thorough Concordance of the LDS Standard Works

A Guide to Publications on the Book of Mormon: A Selected Annotated Bibliography

Book of Mormon Authorship Revisited: The Evidence for Ancient Origins

Ancient Scrolls from the Dead Sea: Photographs and Commentary on a Unique Collection of Scrolls

LDS Perspectives on the Dead Sea Scrolls

Images of Ancient America: Visualizing Book of Mormon Life

Isaiah in the Book of Mormon

King Benjamin's Speech: "That Ye May Learn Wisdom"

Mormons, Scripture, and the Ancient World: Studies in Honor of John L. Sorenson

Latter-day Christianity: Ten Basic Issues

Illuminating the Sermon at the Temple and Sermon on the Mount

Scripture Study: Tools and Suggestions

Finding Biblical Hebrew and Other Ancient Literary Forms in the Book of Mormon

Charting the Book of Mormon: Visual Aids for Personal Study and Teaching

Pressing Forward with the Book of Mormon: The FARMS Updates of the 1990s

King Benjamin's Speech Made Simple

Periodicals

Insights: A Window on the Ancient World

FARMS Review of Books

Journal of Book of Mormon Studies

Reprint Series

Book of Mormon Authorship: New Light on Ancient Origins

The Doctrine and Covenants by Themes

Offenders for a Word

Copublished with Deseret Book Company

An Ancient American Setting for the Book of Mormon

Warfare in the Book of Mormon

By Study and Also by Faith: Essays in Honor of Hugh W. Nibley

The Sermon at the Temple and the Sermon on the Mount

Rediscovering the Book of Mormon

Reexploring the Book of Mormon

Of All Things! Classic Quotations from Hugh Nibley

The Allegory of the Olive Tree

Temples of the Ancient World

Expressions of Faith: Testimonies from LDS Scholars

Feasting on the Word: The Literary Testimony of the Book of Mormon

The Collected Works of Hugh Nibley

Old Testament and Related Studies

Enoch the Prophet

The World and the Prophets

Mormonism and Early Christianity

Lehi in the Desert; The World of the Jaredites; There Were Jaredites

An Approach to the Book of Mormon

Since Cumorah

The Prophetic Book of Mormon

Approaching Zion

The Ancient State

Tinkling Cymbals and Sounding Brass

Temple and Cosmos

Brother Brigham Challenges the Saints

Published through Research Press

Pre-Columbian Contact with the Americas across the Oceans: An Annotated Bibliography

A Comprehensive Annotated Book of Mormon Bibliography

New World Figurine Project, vol. 1

Chiasmus in Antiquity (reprint)

Chiasmus Bibliography

Publications of the FARMS Center for the Preservation of Ancient Religious Texts

The Incoherence of the Philosophers

Dead Sea Scrolls Electronic Reference Library

PREFACE

I have heard remarks in Sunday School class like "Paul is like Isaiah; I don't understand what he is saying" or "Romans is the most difficult and confusing book of the New Testament." Difficulty with Paul's writing, particularly Romans, goes so far that sometimes, in jest, someone will suggest that Paul was perhaps not well informed about the gospel. In addition, as a missionary—both full-time and in the stake—I found Romans used more than any other book of the Bible as evidence that the Church of Jesus Christ of Latter-day Saints teaches false doctrine. For example, many who do not believe that baptism is necessary or who believe that a single act of faith can save them find what they take to be evidence for their positions in Romans.

I write this book in response to both these problems. This book is intended to help Latter-day Saints understand Paul's message in the book of Romans, to help us see that it contains a great deal that is applicable to our situation today. In his letter, Paul teaches what it means to be faithfully obedient, con-trasting faithful obedience with sinfulness and the hypocrisy of mere seeming obedience, both dangers we face today. I have also written this book to show that Paul preaches the same gospel taught by all the prophets—including Isaiah, Habakkuk, Nephi, Jacob, Moroni, Joseph Smith, Spencer W. Kimball, and Gordon B. Hinckley. When we understand Romans, it is obvious that not only need we not fear having others discuss Paul's teachings, but we can use those very teachings to teach the truthfulness of the gospel understood through latter-day revelation. When understood correctly, Romans and the Book of Mormon teach the same things.

A Latter-day Saint might ask, "Why study Romans in particular, and why study one chapter in this much detail?" I have no easy answer except that the New Testament book of Romans has attracted my attention for ten years or more. I have read Romans and reread it; I have thought and written about it. I cannot seem to get it out of my mind, so I have undertaken to write this book, which contains a translation of chapter 1 of the book of Romans to use for comparison to the King James Version (KJV),[1] a discussion of the text of the letter, and a comparison of the contemporary critical Greek text and the King James Version with the Joseph Smith Translation.

Why only chapter 1? A flippant answer might be that it took so many pages to do chapter one that I quit there. A more serious answer is that the kind of reflections found in this book would require perhaps ten large volumes to discuss the entire book of Romans, considerably more than almost any reader would want. However, choosing several excerpts from Romans and discussing them in some detail provides an opportunity to discuss most of the crucial issues of Romans and allows people to use what they feel they have learned from that discussion to think about the rest of Romans on their own. Because it sets the stage for what comes in the following fifteen chapters, Romans 1 is crucial. At present I plan to follow this book with a similar set of reflections on Romans 6–8 and on Romans 12.

Whatever else may also be true, I think it fair to say that the project of writing this book is a result of my religious experience. I converted to the Church of Jesus Christ of Latter-day Saints from Protestantism. (I was a member of the Disciples of Christ.) When I was a Protestant, Paul's letter to the Romans was important to me, though I did not understand it as I now do. It helped me understand what it means to be a Christian. I served a full-time mission and several part-time missions for the LDS Church, and as part of that work I often met with people who preached salvation by faith alone, a doctrine they took from Paul's letter. Talking to them about the letter to the Romans and trying to understand both our agreements and differences was an important part of trying to teach them the ful-

ness of the gospel. Discussing Romans with other Christians has also been an important part of my own spiritual growth and learning; we often turned out to have more in common than either of us thought when we began our discussions.

Romans is important to me because it teaches the doctrine of salvation by grace. I have studied and taught philosophy for more than twenty years, and that study brings me to appreciate more and more the necessity of grace. After many years as a believing member of the church, some time ago I came to better understand the importance of the Book of Mormon, and I began to read and study it more faithfully.[2] As I did so, I saw what I had not expected to see, namely, an emphasis on grace and thus a close connection between the teachings of the Book of Mormon prophets and the teachings of Paul. In addition, my conversion experience, though not publicly dramatic, was a powerful illustration to me of divine grace. I had studied and prayed, but there came a moment when the Spirit bore powerful witness of the truth of the restored gospel in a way that went far beyond what I could have expected based on either my worthiness or even my prayers. I could not but understand that moment as a gift, a moment of grace.

In spite of its length, this work is not in any sense definitive, one that says everything there is to be said about a chapter of scripture. It is not even intended to give a coherent interpretation of part of Paul's letter, much less the best interpretation possible using the resources available. This book is exactly what its subtitle says it is: a collection of notes and reflections on chapter 1 of Romans. The notes tend to be notes about linguistic and cultural matters, notes about details that I hope will help students of the scriptures read and talk with each other about Paul's letter more carefully, notes that may inspire new thought and reflection and, so, new insights. The reflections are ideas that occurred to me as I worked on writing about chapter 1. They are the things I thought about as I studied, so they may be helpful for others who are studying. For example, they may spark similar or related thoughts. Because my reflections are personal, though I try to present evidence for what I say to show that it is not just subjective reflection, others may have very different reactions to or understandings of the passages on which I reflect. (There is a good chance that I will also see things differently on another reading of the same passage.)[3] There is room for difference as well as disagreement in this. My reflections are intended to stimulate thinking and conversation about Romans, not to bring that thinking and conversation to an end by offering oracular or definitive pronouncements about what Paul's letter means.

Of course, the personal nature of my reflections does not relieve me of the responsibility to be accurate. I may make mistakes. Where there are errors, I stand ready to be corrected by those who know more about Greek, about biblical history and exegesis, and about Latter-day Saint (LDS) doctrine. I especially stand ready to be corrected by those who have spiritual authority over me, especially those whom I recognize as apostles of Jesus Christ and prophets of God.

A number of dangers face those who write about scripture. These are the same dangers that face us when we read scripture, but when we write about it, whether we fall prey to those dangers is more publicly manifest. Some of these dangers can be paired with each other for contrast. On the one hand there is the violence of creating unity where there is none. A variety of people wrote our scriptures. Some were prophets and apostles. Others, such as Luke, were interested onlook-ers who seem not to have had relevant ecclesiastical authority. In some cases, such as the book of Job, we do not know who wrote the book. The scriptures were also written at different times in human history, when the Lord's people faced different problems. Because of these varied problems, the scriptures were written in response to different cultural and historical expectations and understandings and in different languages with different possibilities for expression. These kinds of differences suggest that though we must assume that because they come from the same divine source the scriptures are ultimately unified, that unity may not be obvious to us. We may make the unity of the scriptures too easy, assuming not only that the same God has spoken to the prophets throughout the ages, but that our understanding of what he has said is the same as the understanding of previous generations and peoples.

Paired with the danger of forcing unity on the scriptures prematurely or inappropriately is the danger of supplementing the texts that we have, of uncritically adding our personal understanding or the understanding of scholars to the scriptures and then taking our supplements as if they were themselves scripture. We cannot understand what we read, scripture or otherwise, if we do not supplement it with our own understanding and experience, but we must be careful to remember that we are doing so. We must remember that every reading is an interpretation and that every interpretation involves supplementation. However, the logical necessity of interpretation and, therefore, supplementation does not justify the substitution of our interpretations for the scriptures we are reading.

That brings us to another danger: unrecognized supplementation. Sometimes we do violence to the scriptures because they are so familiar to us. We have read some passages so often that we no longer really read them. We pass our eyes over the words. We say the words in our heads or out loud. We talk about and recall passages, but we no longer read them. We no longer allow them to speak to us; we speak for them instead. Reading can be difficult for any number of reasons. One is that the material is difficult to understand. Many find Isaiah difficult in that way. But *reading can also be difficult because it is easy to understand*, for when it is easy, we tend to hear only what we expect, and we may well overlook the things written that could bring us up short.

Paired with this danger of overlooking things because they are too easy is the danger of relying on supposedly canonical interpretations of scripture. Of course, there are canonical interpretations of scripture. The prophets have sometimes interpreted scripture in ways that are doctrinally binding. The First Presidency's 1916 proclamation about the Godhead is a clear example of such canonical interpretation of scripture. Though never officially canonized by the church, the Prophet Joseph Smith's revisions to the King James Bible may also be an example. But many of us go far beyond accepting the words of the prophets. We grow up hearing something taught repeatedly or hear it taught by a favorite teacher, and we assume that what we have heard is doctrinal. We do not search the scriptures to discover the truth of what we have heard (which often does, in fact, turn out to be true). Instead, we allow what we have always been taught to become the standard for what we believe rather than making the scriptures our standard. Then when we read the scriptures, we may force them to conform to that standard, though they may have something different to say to us—or something more that we will miss.

In each of these cases we wrest scripture.

Rather than being wrested by scripture, we twist it to serve our own purposes. There can be no fail-safe method for preventing such wresting, but I have hoped that by attention to details I might help guard myself against it. By thinking about words and phrases rather than trying to bring everything together into a whole, I hope to avoid the temptation to substitute my false unity for the true unity of Paul's letter. The result of that hope is this set of notes and reflections.[4]

As a set of notes and reflections, this work is not a doctrinal exposition, where the word *doctrine* means something like "a systematic set of propositions that describes as completely as possible the beliefs and relations among beliefs held by Latter-day Saints." I am suspicious of that approach to understanding the gospel. I fear that more often than not it puts our interpretations of the teachings of God ahead of those teachings as they appear in the scriptures and the teachings of the latter-day prophets. I think that such an approach implicitly refuses to recognize the scriptures as the standard works.[5] Instead, our ruminations and traditions often become the standard.

Though perhaps this approach is not recognized openly, it seems to me that one common idea of what it means to interpret scripture is to use scripture as a sourcebook for backing up the beliefs we hold. That is a very old idea of what scripture study is, but I think it not too inaccurate to say that it begins to flower in the work of Thomas Aquinas and comes into full bloom only with the rise of Protestant orthodoxy in the seventeenth and eighteenth centuries. It is an idea of scripture study that we Latter-day Saints have commonly adopted from the early Protestants and their modern heirs.[6]

Among academics, a more common kind of scriptural interpretation is one that uses the tools of history and textual history to explain the development of the texts from which we get our scriptures and then uses that historical insight to understand the content of scripture. Though in most ways quite different from what we might call the orthodox approach to scripture, the usual academic approach to scripture shares with the orthodox approach the assumption that we must understand scripture using something outside the scriptures themselves. The supposedly orthodox approach assumes that we must use the systems of beliefs that we already accept, while the academic approach assumes that we must use academic tools. Those different assumptions result in vastly different, even contradicting, interpretations of scripture. But they share the assumption that some system of thought is prior to scripture and that we interpret scripture best when we accommodate it to that system.[7]

I prefer an older, though less common, approach. I prefer to do my best to look to the scriptures themselves and let them teach me their doctrines. The meaning of the word *doctrine* is, after all, "teaching." In this approach, I seek to be taught by scriptures without knowing in advance what they will teach. Rather than beginning by implicitly (or even explicitly) knowing what I will find—by assuming the doctrinal content of the scriptures—I hope to allow the scriptures to teach me. Of course, I would hardly want to deny that I come to Paul's letter to the Romans with preconceptions, ideas, and beliefs. Neither would I want to deny that I use those preconceptions, ideas, and beliefs to help me understand Paul's letter. It is impossible to read and understand even the back of a cereal box, much less something as interesting and fruitful as Romans, without using what we already understand and take to be true. But my goal is to test my beliefs against the texts of scripture rather than to use scripture to justify the beliefs I hold when I come to scripture.

There are times when showing how passages of scripture justify particular beliefs is necessary and important. I doubt that I would have converted to the church had not someone been willing to take that approach with me. On the other hand, there are many things that the academic approach to scripture study can teach us, and it will be obvious that I owe a considerable debt to various scholars for helping me think about Romans. Nevertheless, for most purposes, especially for personal study, I think it is better to come to the scriptures ready to be brought up short—to be questioned and taught in my response to the questions the scriptures ask of me and the demands they make of me. What follows is an attempt to read the first chapter of Paul's letter in that way and to help others to do the same.

As I said earlier, my experience in the church suggests that many of us find Paul's writings, especially the letter to the Romans, intimidating because they are about grace and works and because opponents of the church have often used them to argue that we are doctrinally wrong and even cultic. That is unfortunate, and I hope this book will make some small step toward changing that intimidation. As Edward Schillebeeckx says, "Paul is less concerned with the problem of 'grace' and 'human activity' [i.e., works] than with discovering decisive salvation . . . in the divine gift of Christ Jesus."[8] I want to read Paul's letter and the other scriptures in that same spirit: I want to read them as sermons that preach of Christ rather than as theological treatises, and I hope what I write helps others to read them as such sermons.[9]

Paul's letter to the Romans is sixteen chapters long, and several years of work in my spare time have produced only my response to the first chapter. As a result, I have decided not to write a response to the book of Romans as a whole. The points I think are important can be made in responses to a few chapters. This is my work on the first chapter, a book that I intend to follow with one or two others. Notes and reflections on parts of the book of Romans rather than the whole of it have the advantage of helping to remind readers that they are as prepared and qualified to think about these issues as I am. To that end, I hope readers will respond to my notes and reflections, especially with criticisms or alternative understandings. These thoughts and criticisms will be much appreciated, and they should improve the quality of the notes on chapters that follow. In matters of New Testament study, I am an interested and enthusiastic amateur, not a scholar.

I have already received a great deal of help from many people, from friends and students, from several good teaching assistants, and from colleagues at Brigham Young University. I am grateful to them all and I should thank them by name, but I fear that I will leave someone out. Nevertheless, I am especially grateful to James Siebach, who has spent many hours arguing with me and teaching me how to read. Though I would like to blame any mistakes in this work and any examples of poor judgment on him and the others who have helped me, I have to admit that they are mine. I am also grateful to Daniel B. McKinlay for hours spent cleaning up this manuscript and for conversations about the theological issues raised in Romans 1, and to Larry and Pat Wimmer for being guinea pigs in reading and responding to this work. Thanks are due to those members of the FARMS staff who worked on this manuscript, especially Mary Mahan for her editing and indexing, as well as Josi J. Brewer for her computer work, Robyn Patterson for her source checking, and Jessica Taylor for her proofreading and indexing.

I must also acknowledge that I have relied heavily on the scholarly work of those outside the church. Though I have read many commentaries, Bible dictionaries, grammars, historical works, and other scholarly pieces, I have referred particularly to the commentaries of Cranfield[10] and Fitzmyer,[11] the former a Protestant and the latter a Catholic, because doing so allows me not only to learn from two thoughtful scholars, but also to contrast a Latter-day Saint understanding with representations of the two most common ways of understanding the book of Romans.

Notes

1. Though I have made a new translation of Romans for this commentary, I do not offer it as a stand-alone translation. I intend it to be used along with the edition of the scriptures published by the church in 1981. I offer it to help readers understand more clearly what Romans is saying by giving them something to which to compare the KJV, not to replace the KJV. The KJV is not the only good translation, but its beauty and accuracy make it tough competition for any other translation. Its beauty is such that it has become a classic of literature in its own right, and it is accurate in that it goes out of its way to reproduce the Hebrew and Greek as literally as possible. Sometimes that is part of the reason we have trouble reading it. More often, however, we have trouble because we are not literate enough; we need to know more about our language. The KJV is perhaps most important because it is the translation from which the language of latter-day scriptures comes. If we do not know the King James Bible, we will miss many allusions in latter-day scripture.

2. I remain grateful to Bruce Jorgensen for helping me appreciate the Book of Mormon. His writing about the Book of Mormon (for example, "The Dark Way to the Tree: Typological Unity in the Book Mormon," *Encyclia* 54/2 [1977]: 16–24; reprinted in *Literature of Belief: Sacred Scripture and Religious Experience* [Provo, Utah: BYU Religious Studies Center, 1981], 217–31) was immensely

helpful, but watching him teach students from the Book of Mormon was of even more help.

3. See Dallin H. Oaks, "Scripture Reading and Revelation," *Ensign*, January 1995, 6–9.

4. It should be clear that this is a commentary for laymen, not for scholars. It is unfortunate that there are so few scholarly commentaries on the scriptures and their background by qualified Latter-day Saints, but my training in Greek, Bible history, and so on, is insufficient for me to be able to change that. Instead, this is a commentary by a layman with some background, and it is written for other lay people who do not know Greek but would like to understand more about what the letter to the Romans says without delving into various complexities of word usage or textual problems. This is written for those who might be called to teach the gospel in a Sunday School class or as missionaries, and for anyone who would like some help studying the scriptures more closely.

5. It also implicitly undermines the significance and possibility of continuing revelation, of learning things from the prophets that may radically alter our previous understanding.

6. For more about the varieties of approaches to scriptural interpretation and about the history of those approaches, see Werner E. Lemke and Robert Morgan, "Theology," in *Anchor Bible Dictionary*, ed. David Noel Freedman (New York: Doubleday, 1992), 6:448–83.

7. As noted, both conservative Protestant orthodoxy and contemporary academics share a common assumption, namely, that some metaphysical thing exterior to, logically prior to, the scriptures is essential to understanding them. That assumption is a version of a common belief of the Enlightenment, the belief that everything in this world that can be understood is understood only if there is, standing behind it, a metaphysical entity that gives it meaning and reality. Most twentieth-century philosophy argues that such a belief is difficult or even impossible to make sense of. Without exploring the complexities of that argument, let me simply say that the Latter-day Saint belief that God is an embodied person rather than a metaphysical entity should at least make us suspicious

of that belief. For more on this issue and an alternative view, see my "Scripture as Incarnation," forthcoming in *Historicity and the Latter-day Saint Scriptures*, ed. Paul Y. Hoskisson (Provo, Utah: BYU Religious Studies Center, 2000).

Of course, the situation is also more complicated than my discussion makes it seem: For one thing, the doctrines we believe are relevant to the interpretations of scripture. They often provide a necessary framework for our understanding. For another, it is clear that history is also relevant to our scripture study. The New Testament and the Book of Mormon are radically different documents than they claim to be and they mean something quite different than they claim to mean if they are not, in some strong sense, historical records. Often, not to know something about the culture and practices of New Testament people is not to understand well the documents that make up the New Testament. However, as important as doctrine and history are, neither can be assumed to be the conceptual or metaphysical foundation or standard for our understanding of the scriptures without damaging our understanding that the scriptures are in fact scripture.

8. Edward Schillebeeckx, *Christ: The Experience of Jesus as Lord*, trans. John Bowden (New York: Crossroad, 1980), 146.

9. I suspect that the common interpretation that Paul's letters strongly separate the law of Moses, with its requirement of obedience, from faith is partly a result of anti-Semitism. I see Paul as arguing that the Mosaic law is not sufficient in a context that includes two aspects that he must consider: first, the Pharisees believed that the law of Moses was sufficient, and second, the question had not been settled among first-century Christians (many of whom were Pharisees) and therefore had taken on special urgency as the question of how to deal with gentile converts arose. Later generations took Paul's response to a rhetorical situation and reinterpreted it as a rejection of the necessary connection between obedience and faith. This interpretation was initially strengthened by early Christianity's minority status in Judaism and the feelings that we can speculate

Christians had toward Judaism as they were marginalized and eventually rejected as non-Jewish. It was strengthened even further because of a complex of factors that was and continues to be often an unconscious and sometimes a conscious anti-Semitism. This interpretation existed in spite of the obvious connections of grace and works in first-century Judaism, including even Pharisaism, and in spite of the fact that Paul nowhere disparages the Jews themselves. See Jon D. Levenson, *The Death and Resurrection of the Beloved Son: The Transformation of Child Sacrifice in Judaism and Christianity* (New Haven, Conn.: Yale University Press, 1993), 230.

If I am right, the irony is that in spite of the anti-Semitic origins of this interpretation, even Jews who read the Pauline texts are sometimes guilty of taking up this traditional Christian interpretation that creates a dichotomy between obedience and faith. (Levenson is an example; see *Death and Resurrection*, 219.) Following Christian anti-Semitism, they read something into the text that is not there.

10. See C. E. B. Cranfield, *A Critical and Exegetical Commentary on the Epistle to the Romans*, 6th ed., 2 vols. (Edinburgh: T & T Clark, 1975–79).

11. See Joseph A. Fitzmyer, *Romans: A New Translation with Introduction and Commentary*, The Anchor Bible, vol. 33 (New York: Doubleday, 1993).

I say unto you, if ye have come to a knowledge of the goodness of God, and his matchless power, and his wisdom, and his patience, and his long-suffering towards the children of men; and also, the atonement which has been prepared from the foundation of the world, that thereby salvation might come to him that should put his trust in the Lord, and should be diligent in keeping his commandments, and continue in the faith even unto the end of his life, I mean the life of the mortal body—I say, that this is the man who receiveth salvation, through the atonement which was prepared from the foundation of the world for all mankind, which ever were since the fall of Adam, or who are, or who ever shall be, even unto the end of the world. (Mosiah 4:6–7)

But you, our God, are kind and true, slow to anger, and ruling all with mercy. For even if we sin, we are yours since we acknowledge your power. But we will not sin, knowing that we are accounted yours. For to know you is the perfection of justice, and to recognize your power is the root of immortality. (Wisdom of Solomon 15:1–3)

INTRODUCTION

Romans is a letter written in Greek, the international language of the first century A.D., by Paul to the saints in Rome, probably in the winter or spring of A.D. 55–56. It may have been written in Corinth, just before the journey described in Acts 20 and 21. (Romans 16:23 mentions Gaius, who is perhaps the same person mentioned in 1 Corinthians 1:14 as a resident of Corinth.) Romans 16:22 says that Romans was written by Tertius, but that does not necessarily mean that Paul did not write it. It was common at the time to use scribes to write letters, much as businesspeople often have their secretaries write letters today. Sometimes the person sending the letter would give instructions to the scribe, who would then compose a letter and have it approved before sending. This was a common practice for simple matters, but it is unlikely that something as long and complicated as Romans would have been written this way. Latin writers had a shorthand system that could be used to take dictation, but this was not common, and we have no evidence that a similar system existed in Greek (though it may have), so it is unlikely that the letter was composed in this way. Sometimes, though rarely, authors dictated and scribes wrote down in longhand what they said. Even though this occurred only occasionally, it is quite possible that Romans was composed this way, for this method was used when the subject matter was difficult and it was important that no mistakes be made. In such a case, the author might dictate from a set of notes or an outline of some sort and review the completed letter with the scribe once or more to see that it was the way it should be. Another possibility is that Paul wrote Romans as a letter to several churches, and Tertius was assigned to write a version for each church, inserting the proper references into the text where they were appropriate and adding a list of greetings and other particular matters at the end. This is quite possible and would explain the difficulty of knowing whether Paul was addressing a congregation composed primarily of gentiles or of Jews, a problem that confronts everyone who reads this letter carefully.

One objection to the last explanation is that Paul was the apostle to the gentiles and did not address Jews particularly. That designation, however, seems to be more a geographic designation than a description of whom he taught. After all, to be called on a mission to Italy today is not to be called to teach only those who come from Italy, but to teach those who are in Italy, regardless of their background. Thus, to be called as an apostle to the gentiles would be to be called to teach those who lived among "the nations," as the gentiles were called, not necessarily to teach only those who were not of the house of Israel.

In the end we have no way to know how the letter was composed. But it makes no difference. There is no doubt that it is an authentic letter of Paul, so whether it was written in shorthand or longhand, dictated, or rewritten for several congregations matters little. Some scholars dispute the authorship of various scriptural books. For example, many question whether Paul wrote Hebrews. But no one seriously questions whether Paul is the author of the letter to the Romans. As the LDS Dictionary points out, the letter was written from Corinth to the members in Rome in the mid to late 50s of the first century, and it is the fifth of Paul's extant letters. The books of 1 and 2 Thessalonians, 1 and 2 Corinthians, and Galatians seem to have been written before Romans.

It is not uncommon to hear it said that Paul's style is poor, that he is not a particularly good writer. If that means his letters do not usually conform to the stylistic standards of his day, the standards of classical literary training, it is accurate. But good style is not confined to the style that was common in the schools of Paul's day. Paul has a wide vocabulary and he uses it carefully. He varies his style to suit the subject matter, sometimes using a style similar to what the rabbis used, and sometimes using a style like that found in some of the religious texts that were popular at the time, like Wisdom (also called Wisdom of Solomon). Occasionally he uses the style of Greek rhetoricians, the literary style. Paul's style has much in common with what the Puritans later called plain style. Its grace comes from its simplicity and straightforwardness.

Calling Paul's writing simple may strike many as laughable, but it is accurate. He writes about what are often complicated issues in as simple and straightforward a way as he can without falsifying. The complexity is as much a result of the ideas as it is of the style; for the most part, Paul avoids ornamenting his sentences except with the truth.

On the other hand, as you will see in some of the notes that follow, Paul is not an unsophisticated writer. He knows various literary devices (probably from being a careful listener and reader rather than from formal training in rhetoric), and he uses them effectively and unselfconsciously. Where these literary devices help us understand his point, we will look at how he uses them. Paul is also sophisticated about the ideas of his time. Though there is little reason to believe that he had much classical training, he did receive a good formal Jewish education and, as we will see, he knows many of the ideas of his culture well enough to use them in his letters.

In most of his previous letters, Paul was concerned about particular problems that had arisen in the churches to which he was writing. First Thessalonians is a letter of gratitude and exhortation more than a letter of correction, but 2 Thessalonians, 1 and 2 Corinthians, and Galatians are responses to particular problems of misunderstanding and even apostasy. Paul writes about such things as a too-anxious expectation of the second coming, comfort in the face of persecution, and confusion about—even wholesale defection back to—the Jewish law. In each case Paul writes to congregations he knows personally, congregations created by his missionary work.

However, when Paul writes to the Romans, he writes to those whom he has never visited. As is obvious in the first sixteen verses of chapter 16, Paul knows some individuals in the congregation(s) in Rome. Nevertheless, though he discusses such things as the relation of Jews and gentiles within the church, he does not do so as we would expect him to if he were writing about a particular problem in Rome. He gives no details of any such problems but speaks only generally, perhaps taking up the issue of Jews and gentiles as part of a larger discussion because he knows that the congregation in Rome has large groups of both Jews and gentiles. Thus Romans is a doctrinal exposition rather than a response to a particular problem among the saints in Rome. Nevertheless, as a doctrinal exposition, Paul's letter is not merely an abstract treatise. As he writes, Paul refers to specific errors that people make, explains doctrines in a detailed manner, and uses specific scriptures and examples to explain and justify his teaching.

As we read Romans, it is crucial to remember that Paul is addressing an audience of believers. As a result, we cannot use Romans to decide, for example, whether baptism is required of Christ's followers, because the issue of baptism is not raised in the letter. Nor can we infer an answer about baptism from what Paul says about the law, because he is usually speaking of the Mosaic law in particular and because the audience he was addressing would already have completed whatever prerequisites there were for being counted a Christian. Historical and other scriptural evidence indicates that baptism was required of all early converts to Christianity. Presumably, then, all those to whom Paul is speaking in this letter have been baptized. Consequently, the letter to the Romans could tell us that baptism and similar rites are not required of believers only if it specifically said so, but it does not. I cannot emphasize this point enough: Paul is writing to and for those who are already converted to Christianity. He is preaching to believers to help them understand what it means to be a believer, what they must do and be now that they are converted. Contrary to what some contemporary Protestant ministers teach, Paul is not telling us what one must do to become a Christian.

Paul speaks about a variety of topics in the letter to the Romans. In chapters 9–11, for example, he explains the relation between the house of Israel and the gentiles. Each of the various topics that Paul deals with falls within his overall purpose, which he announces in verses 16 and 17 of chapter 1. Consider the following paraphrase of that message: The preaching of the gospel (and presumably the conversions that result from that preaching) exhibits God's power to save *all*, first the Jew and then the gentile (as is the case in the early church), and the preaching of the gospel exhibits this power because the gospel reveals God's justice and uprightness to those who are faithful, making them more faithful.

Romans is similar to the message that Paul later delivers to the Ephesians:

> Wherefore remember, that ye being in time past Gentiles in the flesh, who are called Uncircumcision by that which is called the Circumcision in the flesh made by hands; That at that time ye were without Christ, being aliens from the commonwealth of Israel, and strangers from the covenants of promise, having no hope,

and without God in the world: But now in Christ Jesus ye who sometimes were far off are made nigh by the blood of Christ. For he is our peace, who hath made both one, and hath broken down the middle wall of partition between us; Having abolished in his flesh the enmity, even the law of commandments contained in ordinances; for to make in himself of twain one new man, so making peace; And that he might reconcile both unto God in one body by the cross, having slain the enmity thereby: And came and preached peace to you which were afar off, and to them that were nigh. For through him we both have access by one Spirit unto the Father. Now therefore ye are no more strangers and foreigners, but fellowcitizens with the saints, and of the household of God; And are built upon the foundation of the apostles and prophets, Jesus Christ himself being the chief corner stone; In whom all the building fitly framed together groweth unto an holy temple in the Lord: In whom ye also are builded together for an habitation of God through the Spirit. (Ephesians 2:11–22)

We who were formerly separated—Jews on one side, gentiles on the other—by the fact that the former had the law of Moses and the latter did not, have now been brought together in faith by Jesus Christ. Having been brought together, we can now grow to be a temple of and in the Lord. Thus it is faith in Jesus Christ that we must preach, and it is faith in Jesus Christ that saves us, not the law of Moses. As Nephi tells us, "It is by grace that we are saved, after all we can do" (2 Nephi 25:23).[1]

Paul's letter to the Romans begins by explaining that all, Jew and gentile, are fallen. All are condemned because of their disobedience to the law, and future obedience to the law cannot make up for past disobedience (see chapters 1–7). That important message is one we must understand if we are to comprehend the importance of repentance and what it means to live by the Spirit. However, that idea is only one part of Paul's message. After insisting that obedience to the law cannot save us, Paul goes on to explain how faith in Jesus Christ can overcome the problem that obedience alone cannot (see chapter 8), namely, our separation from God and our consequent inability to do good. Then, perhaps because of the mixed congregation of Jews and gentiles in Rome, Paul digresses briefly to discuss what this means with regard to the Jews and their relation to the gentiles (see chapters 9–11). Finally, having explained how faith does what mere obedience cannot, Paul explains the place and importance of obedience to the Christian life (see chapters 12–15). He finishes by adding some personal notes directed to the congregation as a whole (see chapter 15) and to specific individuals in Rome (see chapter 16).

The following outline shows the overall structure of the book of Romans:

1. The gospel message (1–11): the gospel has the power to save all (1–8)
   a. God's righteousness assures that those who are faithful will be saved (1:18–4)
      i. All are under condemnation because of sin (1:18–3:20)
      ii. The atonement applies to all equally (3:21–4)
   b. God's love assures the faithful of salvation (5–8)
      i. The Christian life is possible through the Holy Ghost (8)
      ii. Transition to the next major section (which is 12–15)
   c. A doctrinal digression: the relation of the Jews to the gentiles; salvation by faith does not contradict God's promises to Israel (9–11)

2. A Christian's obligations to obedience (12–15)
3. Paul's messages to individual persons (15:13–16:27)

As we read particular passages in Romans, it is helpful to remember this structure and to recall the place of a given passage in that structure. Paul discusses different topics at different times in the letter, but we cannot take what he teaches in one place out of its context in the letter as a whole without changing the meaning of the teaching. Neither can we read one part of the letter as if it were separate from the rest.

Following is the format I have used for my notes and reflections on Romans 1: The text of Romans 1 is divided into five sections that correspond to the paragraphing of the United Bible Societies' *The Greek New Testament*, the Greek text on which I have relied.[2] For example, section 1 discusses verses 1–7, which comprise one paragraph in the Greek text. At the beginning of each sections are two translations of the applicable Greek paragraph in parallel columns. The King James Version is in the left-hand column, and my alternate translation is in the right. (Recall that the alternate translation is provided only as an aid to understanding the language of the KJV; it is not intended to stand on its own.)

Within the exegesis of each section I proceed verse by verse, commenting on the words and phrases within verses in chronological order. The beginning of the exegesis of each verse is marked by the verse number, and the words or phrases I discuss appear before the paragraph that begins the discussion. The KJV provides the anchor point for my exegesis, so the words and phrases are from that translation.

The exegesis of each verse is followed by a comparison of the KJV with the Joseph Smith Translation of the verse. If the Prophet Joseph made no revision, that is noted. Words in the revision that have been added to the KJV or changed in some way are underlined, and deletions are marked by two slashes (/ /) at the point where the deletion occurs.

I hope many will find this commentary helpful to their scripture study. Some may use it only as a reference book. A few may read the work in its entirety. In either case, the point of this work is to help us approach the book of Romans and other scriptures with renewed interest and insight.

After you read whatever portion of my translation and commentary you find helpful, and after you have done whatever other studying of scripture you want to do, I recommend that you finish by reading out loud the King James translation of the passages you have been studying. As a letter, Romans was meant to be read out loud, so reading it that way may give you a better sense of its meaning and how its parts connect to each other. Studying in some detail the construction and meaning of part of Romans will help you read the letter as a whole better—with more meaning—and reading out loud the passages from it that you are studying will often help you better understand what may have been unclear before. Reading out loud may also give you a sense of the passage or letter as a whole, a sense that is sometimes lost when we focus carefully on a small passage or set of passages but that is absolutely essential to understanding Paul's message.

In addition, be sure to read the notes at the bottom of each page in your Bible. Look up the cross-references and the relevant scriptures in the Topical Guide. Compare the emendations made by Joseph Smith to the KJV text and think about the differences these changes make in the meaning. Use the footnotes about Greek words together with this commentary and any other useful translations or commentaries available as study aids; use them to help you understand what Paul means but not to replace reading the letter itself. In short, study the book of Romans and all other scripture with at least as much diligence and care as you might use to study any other good book. (If you have ever had a class in Shakespeare or one in which you learned to read other great literature, many of the study techniques you learned there will help you study the scriptures too. The scriptures are, after all, also the greatest literature.)

My experience tells me that when people study with real intent and seriousness of purpose and heart, they are rewarded. Though spending Sunday afternoon carefully studying the scriptures may not be as easy as just reading through them quickly, it is far more rewarding and, therefore, even far more enjoyable. Truly study the scriptures and you will discover over and over again why the gospel is indeed the good news.

Notes

1. The word *after* usually means "following in time." That meaning yields one possible and common reading of the passage: first we do all that we can, then Christ's grace completes what must be done if we are to be saved. However, the fact that Christ's grace was exhibited in his crucifixion and resurrection, which antedate our works, complicates that reading, though it does not make it impossible. Christ accomplished his act of grace before we did anything. One can also read the word *after* to indicate the relative importance of the two things mentioned, as in the phrase *after all is said and done.* Such a use suggests the insufficiency of what comes first and the fulness or sufficiency of what comes after. I think the latter meaning is more informative as an understanding of 2 Nephi 25:23: we are saved by grace, which is more important than our works.

2. See *The Greek New Testament,* 4th ed., rev. (Stuttgart: United Bible Societies, 1993).

TEXT AND TRANSLATION

ΠΡΟΣ ΡΩΜΑΙΟΥΣ

Κεφάλαιον Α´.

₁Παῦλος δοῦλος Χριστοῦ Ἰησοῦ, κλητὸς ἀπόστολος, ἀφωρισμένος εἰς εὐαγγέλιον θεοῦ, ₂ὃ προεπηγγείλατο διὰ τῶν προφητῶν αὐτοῦ ἐν γραφαῖς ἁγίαις, ₃περὶ τοῦ υἱοῦ αὐτοῦ τοῦ γενομένου ἐκ σπέρματος Δαυὶδ κατὰ σάρκα, ₄τοῦ ὁρισθέντος υἱοῦ θεοῦ ἐν δυνάμει κατὰ πνεῦμα ἁγιωσύνης ἐξ ἀναστάσεως νεκρῶν, Ἰησοῦ Χριστοῦ τοῦ κυρίου ἡμῶν, ₅δι᾽ οὗ ἐλάβομεν χάριν καὶ ἀποστολὴν εἰς ὑπακοὴν πίστεως ἐν πᾶσιν τοῖς ἔθνεσιν ὑπὲρ τοῦ ὀνόματος αὐτοῦ, ₆ἐν οἷς ἐστε καὶ ὑμεῖς κλητοὶ Ἰησοῦ Χριστοῦ, ₇πᾶσιν τοῖς οὖσιν ἐν Ῥώμῃ ἀγαπητοῖς θεοῦ, κλητοῖς ἁγίοις· χάρις ὑμῖν καὶ εἰρήνη ἀπὸ θεοῦ πατρὸς ἡμῶν καὶ κυρίου Ἰησοῦ Χριστοῦ.

₈Πρῶτον μὲν εὐχαριστῶ τῷ θεῷ μου διὰ Ἰησοῦ Χριστοῦ περὶ πάντων ὑμῶν, ὅτι ἡ πίστις ὑμῶν καταγγέλλεται ἐν ὅλῳ τῷ κόσμῳ. ₉μάρτυς γάρ μού ἐστιν ὁ θεός, ᾧ λατρεύω ἐν τῷ πνεύματί μου ἐν τῷ εὐαγγελίῳ τοῦ υἱοῦ αὐτοῦ, ὡς ἀδιαλείπτως μνείαν ὑμῶν ποιοῦμαι

Author's Translation

₁Paul, a bondman of Jesus Christ, one called as an apostle, one set apart to the gospel of God—₂the gospel that he had promised previously through his prophets, in the holy scriptures ₃and that is about his Son, who is from the seed of David according to the flesh ₄but who was powerfully appointed to be the Son of God; in other words, he was appointed in accord with the spirit of holiness, by the resurrection of the dead (namely, Jesus Christ our Lord, ₅through whom we received the grace of apostleship to bring about, for his name's sake, trusting obedience among all the gentiles, ₆among whom you are also called of Jesus Christ)—₇to all that are in Rome, beloved of God and called as saints: grace to you and peace from God, our Father, and the Lord Jesus Christ.

₈Chiefly, I thank my God through Jesus Christ for all of you, because your faith is spoken of in the whole world. ₉God, whom I serve spiritually in preaching the gospel of his Son, is my witness of how I mention you

₁₀πάντοτε ἐπὶ τῶν προσευχῶν μου, δεόμενος
εἴ πως ἤδη ποτὲ εὐοδωθήσομαι ἐν τῷ θελήματι
τοῦ θεοῦ ἐλθεῖν πρὸς ὑμᾶς. ₁₁ἐπιποθῶ γὰρ
ἰδεῖν ὑμᾶς, ἵνα τι μεταδῶ χάρισμα ὑμῖν
πνευματικὸν εἰς τὸ στηριχθῆναι ὑμᾶς, ₁₂τοῦτο
δέ ἐστιν συμπαρακληθῆναι ἐν ὑμῖν διὰ τῆς
ἐν ἀλλήλοις πίστεως ὑμῶν τε καὶ ἐμοῦ. ₁₃οὐ
θέλω δὲ ὑμᾶς ἀγνοεῖν, ἀδελφοί, ὅτι πολλάκις
προεθέμην ἐλθεῖν πρὸς ὑμᾶς, καὶ ἐκωλύθην
ἄχρι τοῦ δεῦρο, ἵνα τινὰ καρπὸν σχῶ καὶ ἐν
ὑμῖν καθὼς καὶ ἐν τοῖς λοιποῖς ἔθνεσιν.
₁₄Ἕλλησίν τε καὶ βαρβάροις, σοφοῖς τε καὶ
ἀνοήτοις ὀφειλέτης εἰμί· ₁₅οὕτως τὸ κατ'
ἐμὲ πρόθυμον καὶ ὑμῖν τοῖς ἐν Ῥώμῃ
εὐαγγελίσασθαι.

₁₆Οὐ γὰρ ἐπαισχύνομαι τὸ εὐαγγέλιον,
δύναμις γὰρ θεοῦ ἐστιν εἰς σωτηρίαν παντὶ
τῷ πιστεύοντι, Ἰουδαίῳ τε πρῶτον καὶ
Ἕλληνι· ₁₇δικαιοσύνη γὰρ θεοῦ ἐν αὐτῷ
ἀποκαλύπτεται ἐκ πίστεως εἰς πίστιν, καθὼς
γέγραπται· Ὁ δὲ δίκαιος ἐκ πίστεως
ζήσεται.

₁₈Ἀποκαλύπτεται γὰρ ὀργὴ θεοῦ ἀπ'
οὐρανοῦ ἐπὶ πᾶσαν ἀσέβειαν καὶ ἀδικίαν
ἀνθρώπων τῶν τὴν ἀλήθειαν ἐν ἀδικίᾳ
κατεχόντων, ₁₉διότι τὸ γνωστὸν τοῦ θεοῦ
φανερόν ἐστιν ἐν αὐτοῖς· ὁ θεὸς γὰρ αὐτοῖς
ἐφανέρωσεν. ₂₀τὰ γὰρ ἀόρατα αὐτοῦ ἀπὸ
κτίσεως κόσμου τοῖς ποιήμασιν νοούμενα
καθορᾶται, ἥ τε ἀΐδιος αὐτοῦ δύναμις καὶ
θειότης, εἰς τὸ εἶναι αὐτοὺς ἀναπολογήτους·
₂₁διότι γνόντες τὸν θεὸν οὐχ ὡς θεὸν ἐδόξασαν
ἢ ηὐχαρίστησαν, ἀλλ' ἐματαιώθησαν ἐν τοῖς
διαλογισμοῖς αὐτῶν καὶ ἐσκοτίσθη ἡ ἀσύνετος
αὐτῶν καρδία. ₂₂φάσκοντες εἶναι σοφοὶ
ἐμωράνθησαν, ₂₃καὶ ἤλλαξαν τὴν δόξαν τοῦ
ἀφθάρτου θεοῦ ἐν ὁμοιώματι εἰκόνος φθαρτοῦ
ἀνθρώπου καὶ πετεινῶν καὶ τετραπόδων καὶ
ἑρπετῶν.

₂₄Διὸ παρέδωκεν αὐτοὺς ὁ θεὸς ἐν ταῖς
ἐπιθυμίαις τῶν καρδιῶν αὐτῶν εἰς ἀκαθαρσίαν
τοῦ ἀτιμάζεσθαι τὰ σώματα αὐτῶν ἐν αὐτοῖς,
₂₅οἵτινες μετήλλαξαν τὴν ἀλήθειαν τοῦ θεοῦ

unceasingly; ₁₀always in my prayers I ask
whether now, at last, I will be blessed by
God's will to come to you. ₁₁For I long to see
you so that I can share some spiritual gift
with you so that you may be strengthened.
₁₂This gift is that I will be strengthened with
you through the trust we share, your trust
and mine. ₁₃However, I do not wish you to be
ignorant, brothers: I often intended to come
to you so that I might have some fruit among
you, too, even as I have had among the other
gentiles, but I was prevented until the present.
₁₄I am a debtor to Greeks and non-Greeks, to
the wise and the foolish; ₁₅thus, for my part, I
am eager to preach the gospel also to you in
Rome.

₁₆I am not ashamed of the gospel; for it is
God's power to bring salvation for all those
who are trusting, to the Jew first and to the
Greek. ₁₇For through trust, God's justice is revealed by the gospel to those who trust, even
as it has been written: "And the just will live
by trust."

₁₈For God's wrath is revealed from heaven
against all the impiety and injustice of those
who suppress the truth by injustice. ₁₉This
occurs because that which is known about
God is manifest in them, for God made it
manifest in them. ₂₀Since the creation of the
world, his unseen attributes, both his eternal
power and his divinity, are perceived when
they are understood by means of his works.
Thus, such persons are without excuse
₂₁because, although they knew God, they did
not glorify him as God, nor were they thankful. Instead, they were brought to futility in
their speculations, and their undiscerning
hearts were darkened. ₂₂Claiming to be wise,
they became foolish, ₂₃and they exchanged
the glory of the incorruptible God for the
likeness of an image of corruptible man, and
of birds, and of beasts, and of reptiles.

₂₄For this reason, God abandoned them in

ἐν τῷ ψεύδει, καὶ ἐσεβάσθησαν καὶ ἐλάτρευσαν
τῇ κτίσει παρὰ τὸν κτίσαντα, ὅς ἐστιν
εὐλογητὸς εἰς τοὺς αἰῶνας· ἀμήν. ₂₆διὰ
τοῦτο παρέδωκεν αὐτοὺς ὁ θεὸς εἰς πάθη
ἀτιμίας· αἵ τε γὰρ θήλειαι αὐτῶν μετήλλαξαν
τὴν φυσικὴν χρῆσιν εἰς τὴν παρὰ φύσιν,
₂₇ὁμοίως τε καὶ οἱ ἄρσενες ἀφέντες τὴν
φυσικὴν χρῆσιν τῆς θηλείας ἐξεκαύθησαν ἐν
τῇ ὀρέξει αὐτῶν εἰς ἀλλήλους, ἄρσενες ἐν
ἄρσεσιν τὴν ἀσχημοσύνην κατεργαζόμενοι
καὶ τὴν ἀντιμισθίαν ἣν ἔδει τῆς πλάνης
αὐτῶν ἐν ἑαυτοῖς ἀπολαμβάνοντες. ₂₈καὶ
καθὼς οὐκ ἐδοκίμασαν τὸν θεὸν ἔχειν ἐν
ἐπιγνώσει, παρέδωκεν αὐτοὺς ὁ θεὸς εἰς
ἀδόκιμον νοῦν, ποιεῖν τὰ μὴ καθήκοντα,
₂₉πεπληρωμένους πάσῃ ἀδικίᾳ πονηρίᾳ
πλεονεξίᾳ κακίᾳ, μεστοὺς φθόνου φόνου
ἔριδος δόλου κακοηθείας, ψιθυριστάς,
₃₀καταλάλους, θεοστυγεῖς, ὑβριστάς,
ὑπερηφάνους, ἀλαζόνας, ἐφευρετὰς κακῶν,
γονεῦσιν ἀπειθεῖς, ₃₁ἀσυνέτους, ἀσυνθέτους,
ἀστόργους, ἀνελεήμονας· ₃₂οἵτινες τὸ
δικαίωμα τοῦ θεοῦ ἐπιγνόντες, ὅτι οἱ τὰ
τοιαῦτα πράσσοντες ἄξιοι θανάτου εἰσίν, οὐ
μόνον αὐτὰ ποιοῦσιν ἀλλὰ καὶ συνευδοκοῦσιν
τοῖς πράσσουσιν.

the lusts of their hearts to uncleanness that
they might dishonor their bodies with one
another; ₂₅they exchanged the truth of God
for the lie and worshipped and served the
created thing in place of the Creator, who is
to be praised for eternity. Amen. ₂₆This is why
God gave them over to dishonorable pas-
sions: even their females changed the natural
use to that against nature. ₂₇In the same way,
the males, having forsaken the natural use of
the female, burned up in their lust toward
one another, males acting out shamefulness
among males, and receiving in return the reward that was appropriate to their self-deceit.
₂₈Just as they did not think it fit to maintain a
knowledge of God, God left them to an unfit
mind, to do the things that are improper:
₂₉having been filled with all injustice, malice,
insatiability, and vice; full of envy, murder,
quarrels, deceit, and conspiracy; being gossips,
₃₀slanderers, God-haters, over-reaching, proud,
braggarts, devisers of evil, disobedient to
parents, ₃₁undiscerning, covenant breaking,
unloving, and unmerciful—₃₂they are they
who, having known the judgment of God,
namely, that those who practice such things
are worthy of death, not only do them, but
also approve of those who practice them.

Verses 1–7

King James

₁Paul, a servant of Jesus Christ, called to be an apostle, separated unto the gospel of God, ₂(Which he had promised afore by his prophets in the holy scriptures,) ₃Concerning his Son Jesus Christ our Lord, which was made of the seed of David according to the flesh; ₄And declared to be the Son of God with power, according to the spirit of holiness, by the resurrection from the dead: ₅By whom we have received grace and apostleship, for obedience to the faith among all nations, for his name: ₆Among whom are ye also the called of Jesus Christ: ₇To all that be in Rome, beloved of God, called to be saints: Grace to you and peace from God our Father, and the Lord Jesus Christ.

Alternate[1]

₁Paul, a bondman of Jesus Christ, one called as an apostle, one set apart to the gospel of God—₂the gospel that he had promised previously through his prophets, in the holy scriptures ₃and that is about his Son, who is from the seed of David according to the flesh ₄but who was powerfully appointed to be the Son of God; in other words, he was appointed in accord with the spirit of holiness, by the resurrection of the dead (namely, Jesus Christ our Lord, ₅through whom we received the grace of apostleship to bring about, for his name's sake, trusting obedience among all the gentiles, ₆among whom you are also called of Jesus Christ)—₇to all that are in Rome, beloved of God and called as saints: grace to you and peace from God, our Father, and the Lord Jesus Christ.

Paul, a servant of Jesus Christ, called to be an apostle, separated unto the gospel of God,

Verse 1

Most Greek letters of New Testament times began, "Claudius to Gaius, greeting," using the names of the sender and the addressee in the appropriate places (see, for example, James 1:1; Acts 15:23; 23:26). Similarly, writers of Jewish letters usually began, "Joshua to Judah, peace be multiplied," using the appropriate names (see Daniel 4:1).[2] All the letters in the New Testament except Hebrews and 1 John begin with a variation of the standard Jewish opening. (Partly because Hebrews and 1 John do not begin in that way, we may question whether they were written as letters.) In addition to Romans, ten of the letters begin with "——— to ———, grace and peace be multiplied" or something similar (see 1 and 2 Corinthians; Galatians; Ephesians; Philippians; 1 and 2 Thessalonians; Philemon; 1 and 2 Peter). Four begin, "——— to ———, grace, mercy, and peace be multiplied" (see 1 and 2 Timothy; Titus; 2 John). Jude begins, "Jude . . . to them that are sanctified by God the Father, and preserved in Jesus Christ, and called: Mercy unto you, and peace, and love, be multiplied," a slight variation of the beginning seen in the other letters. James uses the standard Roman beginning, while 3 John names the writer and the addressee but uses no benediction.

The greetings of these letters were often expanded. First Peter, for example, expands the greeting, as many other letters do, by describing both the writer and the addressee in some detail: "Peter, an apostle of Jesus Christ, to the strangers scattered throughout Pontus, Galatia, Cappadocia, Asia, and Bithynia, Elect according to the foreknowledge of God the Father, through sanctification of the Spirit, unto obedience and sprinkling of the blood of Jesus Christ: Grace unto you, and peace, be multiplied" (1 Peter 1:1–2). In Romans, Paul uses the most common greeting (certainly the one that characterizes his letters), but he expands it considerably more than the writers of the other letters do, taking the first six verses to say whom the letter is from. He introduces Galatians with a similar expanded greeting, though not as long. In Galatians the longer introduction seems to serve as a way of refuting what those who opposed his ministry to the gentiles said about him (see Galatians 1:6–2:21). The introduction to the letter to the Romans may have the same intent (see below, *called*, page 10). There seems to have been some controversy in the early church about Paul's status in the church, a question that is not surprising given the way Paul was called and his conduct prior to that call (see Acts 9; 22). However, the beginning of Romans is not clearly a response to that controversy.

Paul writes the other letters of which we have record to churches where he had preached and had personal and ecclesiastical authority. Though Rome fell within his apostolic jurisdiction as the apostle to the gentiles, Paul had never been to Rome. Consequently, in addition to making his ecclesiastical authority clear, he may have felt more than the usual need to justify sending the Romans a letter such as this. Verses 10–13 seem to support this view.

Paul

Traditionally Paul's two names, Paul and Saul, have been explained by the Christian custom of changing one's name upon baptism. That tradition, which may or may not have been practiced in the early church, presumes that Paul was known as Saul until his conversion and then changed his name to Paul afterwards. However, the book of Acts does not support such an explanation. In Acts he is called Saul after his conversion (see Acts 13:1) and when the name Paul is introduced, no reason is given. It is simply mentioned as another name by which he is known (see Acts 13:9). Naming customs of the time may explain this.

Having three names was a mark of Roman citizenship.[3] Those names were a personal name (praenomen), a clan name (nomen), and a family name (cognomen). In addition, it was not unusual for people to have a nickname (supernomen). Paulus, of which the Greek Paulos (Παῦλος, Paul in English) is a variant, was a common Roman family name. It never occurs as a personal name in other documents from Paul's time,[4] so it is highly doubtful that it was Paul's personal name. On the other hand, Saul was a relatively common Jewish personal name. Saul could have been Paul's personal name or his nickname. Thus the two names seem to be just that, two different ways of identifying Paul, much as one could identify me as Faulconer or as James or as Jim.

Why does Acts use the name Saul more in the beginning of its discussion of Paul and the name Paul more later on, and why do most scriptural references refer to him as Paul? One explanation is that the Bible may use the personal name Saul more in reference to Paul's activities among the Jews, and his Roman family name, Paul, more for his work among the gentiles, where Roman custom was more influential. Since Paul's calling was to the gentiles and the extant letters are to congregations among the gentiles, if this hypothesis is correct, we would expect to see more use of his Roman name than his Jewish one, as we do.

A servant of Jesus Christ

A servant of Jesus Christ is a phrase New Testament letter writers commonly used to describe themselves. (Besides Paul's use of the phrase in Galatians 1:10 and Titus 1:1, see James 1:1; 2 Peter 1:1; Jude 1:1.) Jesus describes the believer's relation to God as that of a servant (see Matthew 24:45–51; Luke 12:37–40). The word servant and related words (for example, serve) are especially important in Paul's vocabulary. (In addition to Romans 1:1, see 1:9, 25; 6:6, 16–17, 20; 7:6, 25; 8:15, 21; 9:4, 12; 12:1, 11; 14:18; 16:18.)

The Greek word translated "servant" is doulos (δοῦλος). Literally, it means "slave." However, since slavery in Paul's day was often not accompanied by the cruelty that contemporary Americans usually associate with it, "slave" is not quite right as a translation for us.[5] On the other hand, the word servant is probably too weak for what Paul means, since for him the word's primary connotation is compulsory service by a person who is absolutely dependent on and belongs to the master of a household (using belongs in its strong, economic sense). In Paul's day, douloi (servants) were property, in other words, slaves. In principle, during the first century A.D. the master of the house controlled, was responsible for, and had authority over everything about the slave, up to and including his or her life.[6] As chapter 8 suggests, the slave that Paul has in mind is not of the lowest class and most common kind of slaves, those who do menial work. Many menial slaves may have lived under harsh conditions.[7] Instead, he seems to have in mind the slaves who managed the affairs of their masters and who were sometimes freed or adopted into the family of the master.

Paul uses the word translated "servant" in a complicated context. His use of the word is in part determined by the way it is used in other scriptures. It is also determined by the conventions surrounding Greek, Roman, and Jewish slavery in his own time, as well as by

> Paul, a servant of Jesus Christ, called to be an apostle, separated unto the gospel of God,

the ideals of the various cultures in which he finds himself immersed, ideals that do not always square with common practice. Given his rabbinic training, Paul is surely as dependent on the Old Testament understanding of slavery as he is on the meanings of the Greek word he uses here; the members of his audience who are familiar with the Old Testament almost certainly have its use of the word in mind, along with the Greek and Roman connotations resulting from the dominance of those cultures. In fact, though Paul could not be unaware of Greek procedures for freeing slaves (see 1 Corinthians 7:20–22), he does not use the language of those practices, such as is found in the inscriptions at Delphi.[8]

In contrast to what the Jews in Paul's audience would have understood, converts probably knew little about the scriptural traditions associated with the word *doulos* and likely depended almost entirely on the cultural practices and ideals of Paul's day for their understanding of slavery and its associated practices. Consequently, when we wish to understand what Paul means by *servant*, we must keep in mind both the Old Testament use of the corresponding Hebrew word and the Greek and Roman concepts of what it means to be a slave.

Using language that is common in ancient Near Eastern religion,[9] the Old Testament describes the prophets as God's servants, as in Amos 3:7, "Surely the Lord God will do nothing, but he revealeth his secret unto his servants the prophets," and Isaiah 53:11, where Christ is called "my righteous servant." (The Hebrew word for *servant* is עֶבֶד, *'ebed*; see such passages as Joshua 14:7; 24:29; Judges 2:8; 2 Kings 17:23; Psalms 89:3; 105:6, which suggest that the word *servant* was used for special

ministers rather than just for anyone.) The Septuagint (a third-century-B.C. translation of the Old Testament into Greek made from a manuscript that is no longer extant, also the Bible that Paul seems to use most) uses closely related Greek words in Amos 3:7 and Isaiah 53:11 (meaning "slave" and "to be a slave," respectively). The word used in Amos 3:7 is *doulos*, the same word used by Paul in Romans 1:1. (For more about the Septuagint, see the discussion of verse 17, pages 65–66.)

The Greek word *doulos* is also common in the New Testament. It is one of a number of Greek words that can be translated "slave" or "servant," but it emphasizes the dependence of the slave on his or her master.[10] According to the New Testament, all Christians are slaves (see, for example, Matthew 6:24; Luke 12:41–46; Revelation 19:5).[11] In fact, the word *doulos* may have been an early general title for church leaders, comparable to our use of *Elder*.[12] In addition to the connotations of prophecy and temple service that carry over from *slave* (*servant* in the King James Version [KJV]) as it is used in the Old Testament to refer to the prophets, the New Testament use of the word adds the connotation of the service one owes to one's fellows, as in Matthew 24:45–46; 25:21; Mark 10:42–45. We can expect the following meanings to come together in Paul's use of the word *doulos*: "prophecy" (including and perhaps primarily the preaching of the gospel) and "service" (to one's fellows and even in the temple).

Though the Old Testament makes provisions for the emancipation of slaves at regular periods (see Exodus 21:2–6; Leviticus 25:39–42; 47–54), the Jewish law of Paul's time classed non-Jewish slaves as immobile property. Such slaves had no rights and could not own property.[13] Among Jews of Paul's time, to be called a slave was to be insulted as severely as possible; in fact, calling someone a slave could result in excommunication.[14] Greek and therefore Roman ideals concerning slavery were similar and complicated.[15] A slave was the property of another and owed his owner work. (That the slave was property may well account for the fact that many of the metaphors Paul uses in Romans are economic, including many words from bookkeeping, or legal.) Though slavery was common, according to Greek and Roman conventional wisdom of the time, to be enslaved was repugnant. It was so repugnant, in fact, that some readers of the New Testament may find it difficult to take seriously Paul's use of the word *slave* in Romans 1:1. For them, Paul would have to mean something different than what his contemporary Greek speakers meant. As I will argue, this approach goes too far, ignoring the Hebrew background within which Paul uses the word *slave* and the doctrine that Paul preaches.

For Greek thinkers, and therefore for all the Mediterranean world at the time, nothing seemed worse for a human to endure than being enslaved. The point of Greek and Roman philosophy was to make freedom possible. The Stoic philosopher Epictetus taught that the point of existence was to be free, and he argued that philosophic wisdom gave one that freedom: "What makes a person free from hindrance and gives a person self rule? . . . The knowledge of how to live."[16] For the Stoic, those who are wise are not slaves, no matter what their social state, while those who are not wise are slaves. The Greek word *autonomia* (αὐτονομία), like the English word derived from it (*autonomy*), means "independence." Literally, it means "self-rule." To the Greeks and Romans of Paul's day, autonomy was the chief goal for human beings: "One is free who lives according to his or her decisions, who is subject neither to necessity nor hindrance, nor force, whose desires are un-

hindered, whose longings are fulfilled, whose dislikes do not come to pass."[17] For the Stoic, even though one may have no control over certain events or circumstances, such as being physically enslaved or having a physical disability, one always has control of one's thoughts and desires. Those who live wisely rule their thoughts and desires, even in the face of what appear to be conditions that coerce them. No one is their master. They rule themselves by ruling their minds and controlling their desires. According to the Stoic, that is what it means to be free.

Such an understanding of freedom may seem quite modern to us. We often see parallels between Stoicism and Christianity, for example, in the Stoic emphasis on moderation and in the Stoic belief in God. On the issue of freedom, however, the contrast between Stoic philosophy and Paul's understanding is immense. When Paul calls himself a slave—a person ruled absolutely by another—he says something shocking, both to us and to his original audience. It was perhaps especially shocking to anyone who, like his audience, was living in Rome, the cultural and political center of the Mediterranean, where Stoic ideas were so common that they were often considered simple common sense. In fact, they were so obvious that they seemed impossible to contradict.[18] But, as we will see, Paul is purposely denying his autonomy, and his letter to the Romans makes it clear that he is denying not only his physical autonomy but—more importantly—his mental and spiritual autonomy. In declaring himself a slave, Paul sets himself squarely against the beliefs of most of his contemporaries and many of us, and he declares that his life is not his own in any way. Paul, unlike the Stoic, argues that true Christians, the people most developed as human beings, are ruled not by themselves, but by Another.

> Paul, a servant of Jesus Christ, called to be an apostle, separated unto the gospel of God,

Paul's understanding of slavery and of his relation to both the Father and the Son makes it entirely appropriate for him to call himself a slave of Christ. Similarly, it is also fitting to think of ourselves as Christ's slaves (though perhaps, given the use of the term *slave* to refer to the prophets and the Son, we should instead aspire to be slaves rather than claim already to be slaves). One way to put the central question of this letter is, What does it mean to be owned by God? At least in part, the answer is that Christ bought us through his sacrifice and we are therefore indebted to him: we owe him our work because we owe him our very selves. He owns us. Paul's slavery is his answer to the call given to him through the gospel.

This notion of being owned by Christ is the source of much of what is commonly misunderstood in Paul's writings, namely, the idea that we are saved not by works, but by grace. If we think about our works as Paul does, then works are not what we do to earn our salvation, for a slave can earn nothing. A slave works, but by definition, a slave works without being paid; he or she works without earning anything.[19] Thus, if we follow this understanding of what it means to be a slave of God, our works are what we do because we have become the servants, or bondmen and bondwomen, of Jesus Christ. Our works are what we owe him because he owns us; he has bought us with a price, so we are obliged to serve him. If we do not perform the works he requires then we are rebellious slaves, refusing to do what we ought, what we owe. If we do perform that service, when he gives us something, such as a present or gift of grace and kindness, it is not because we have earned it by our work. We do not earn a re-

ward for doing what we are already obliged to do, for trying to pay back what we owe but, as King Benjamin reminds us, can never pay back (see Mosiah 2:24; see also Luke 17:7–10). Rather, we receive the reward because the Lord (in other words, our master, he who owns us) is a kind and merciful and loving lord, or owner. In these first words of his letter to the Romans, Paul introduces what will become a major theme in his letter, namely, how what we owe God is related to what God gives us.

Sometimes as we read Paul or other ancient writers, we may be tempted to read our own understanding of things into their work. For example, when we read Romans, we may wonder about free will and how it fits into Paul's explanations, or when we read about free agency, we may assume that those words mean the same thing we mean by "free will." We sometimes seem to think that our way of thinking is the only one, that our ideas are the standard by which all ideas should be judged. However, Paul's metaphor of the servant explicitly questions our ideas about freedom.

At least since the Enlightenment we have followed the Greeks in placing a high value on freedom and autonomy. The idea of a rational agent freely choosing and defining himself or herself by individual choices is an important part of our understanding of what it means to be a person.[20] Thus we are likely to be as scandalized by Paul calling himself a slave as the Greek philosophers of Paul's day would have been. However, our idea of free will is not shared by ancient Near Eastern religions, and it is clearly not an idea Paul holds. In direct contrast to the Greek philosophical ideas that have become so important to us, Paul's understanding of what it means to be a person has little or no place for the notion of a rational agent or self-definition. When Paul calls himself a servant or slave, he does not think of himself as defined by a choice he has made. Perhaps Paul could claim to be defined by the simple but important choice to obey rather than to disobey (compare 2 Nephi 2:27). However, even those who choose to disobey are defined by their disobedience. They are negatively defined by their relation to the Savior, but they are not self-defining. Paul is defined by the one who rules him, by Christ rather than by himself. It is precisely Paul's lack of choice that makes him who he is. As he says in 1 Corinthians 9:16, "For though I preach the gospel, I have nothing to glory of: for *necessity is laid upon me*; yea, woe is unto me, if I preach not the gospel!" (emphasis added).[21] In a very real sense Paul does not choose to serve Christ but is required to do so by his experience on the road to Damascus. He owes that service; he *must* serve. Choosing to obey because of his experience gives him no other real choice; Paul now has no more choices to make, for a slave is one who does the will of another rather than his own. According to this line of thought, if each of my acts is a matter of my free will, a matter of personal choice and self-definition—in other words, if I am autonomous —my obedience is idolatry, for I am the ruler whom I obey, the lord and master, and God is not. I set myself up as equal in authority to the Divine, even if what I choose to do is in accord with what he would have me do. Surely Paul would be as scandalized by such idolatrous autonomy as we are by his rejection of autonomy.[22]

An interesting question arises regarding both Christ's promise in John 15:15 that the twelve apostles will henceforth be his friends, not his slaves, and what Paul thinks about slavery. John clearly shares with Paul the understanding that a Christian's relation to Christ is a relation of service, even of servitude, but it is not clear what it means to be a friend of God. Although I risk reading too much into Paul's categories, let me suggest that Romans 8 offers an answer to the question. There Paul explains that we are to become the children of God (see 8:16). Perhaps that is also a discussion of how we become his friends. In chapters 7 and 8, Paul seems to identify three categories of people: (1) the nonslaves or supposedly free, in other words, those who have not yet taken the name of Christ on themselves; (2) the slaves, namely, those who have joined the church and become Christ's slaves by covenant; and (3) the children, those who have been sanctified or adopted and brought back into the family of God to become children of God.

Under Greco-Roman law, a valued slave could be adopted into the family rather than simply emancipated.[23] (As Exodus 21:2–6 shows, the Hebrews had an analogous practice.) In fact, there were definite advantages to being adopted rather than emancipated, chiefly the possible right of inheritance. On the other hand, there were close similarities between children and slaves in Greek and Roman cultures. The word *pais* (παῖς) can mean either "child" (specifically "son") or "slave."[24] Both Greek and Roman fathers had enormous power over their children: a Roman father had absolute right over his sons until he died. For example, in principle he could order that his children be exposed at birth so that they would die. He could order adult children to execute themselves or to expose their own children.[25] Technically, children, even adult children, had no rights before their fathers. However, it is also true that fathers were expected to treat their children and slaves with kindness; fathers had a moral obligation to their slaves even if they had no legal obligation.[26]

Paul seems to be using the similarities of children and slaves to make his point. His use of the word *slave* and his chapter 8 discussion

> Paul, a servant of Jesus Christ, called to be an apostle, separated unto the gospel of God,

of becoming the children of God seem to me to point to the very center of Paul's message: living in a fallen world, we are slaves either to God or to sin. If we are slaves to sin, we will reap only death. If we are faithful slaves to the Father, he will make us his children once again and give us an inheritance with his Son. (Compare this to Lehi's sermon in 2 Nephi 2:27–29.) As Martin has pointed out, the idea of slavery in the New Testament connotes not only obedience, but salvation.[27] Paul's letter to the Romans will show us how that is the case.

In the meantime, since we have not yet been adopted into the divine family, being slaves of God is no small thing. The use of the word *slave* reflects a parallel with the use of slavery in the Old Testament, where, as mentioned, the prophets are called slaves (for example, in Joshua 14:7; 24:29). The prophets are slaves to God, but that slavery gives them a great deal of power, authority, and responsibility. Precisely because they are slaves, what they do is accomplished by the authority of God. This transfer of power from the lord to the slave is paralleled in the practice of slavery among Greeks and Romans during Paul's time. Greek and Roman slaves, especially the slaves of powerful persons, such as the emperor, often had power, wealth, and even social status of their own because they served a powerful person. These slaves administered accounts, sometimes had free persons in their employ, and bought and sold property both for themselves and for their masters. These ancient stewards were often trusted so much that they were allowed to function, for all intents and purposes, as if they were free, though they were in charge of and responsible for the property of their master and were legally the

agents of their masters rather than of themselves.[28] In addition to the other connections Paul makes by calling himself a slave, he shows his relation to the Father and the Son: he is their steward and agent, one who manages the earthly affairs of the divine household.

Similarly, by referring to himself as a slave, Paul may also be drawing a parallel between his own work and that of Christ. (Recall that Isaiah 53:11 speaks of Christ as a servant, a slave if translated literally.) Writing to the Philippians and speaking of Christ, Paul says, "Who, existing in the form of God, did not think to cling to equality with God, but emptied himself, taking upon himself the form of a slave and being born in the likeness of a human being" (Philippians 2:6–7; author's translation). This verse is worthy of considerable comment. Such things as the contrast between the form of God and the likeness of human beings and the contrast between clinging ("robbery" in the KJV) and emptying oneself ("made himself of no reputation" in the KJV) beg thought and discussion. However, I draw attention only to Jesus' taking on himself the form of a slave. The word used here for *form* (*morphē*, μορφή) most often means "outward appearance" or "shape," but since it contrasts the form of God with the likeness of humans in this verse and since Paul speaks of the form of a slave, which is not a matter of shape or outward appearance, Paul must be referring to something other than outward appearance or shape.

Paul hints at what he means by the word *form* in Galatians 4:19, where he says he will work with the Galatians "until Christ be formed in you." In that phrase we see further evidence that *form* means more than "outward appearance," and we also see evidence for the earlier suggestion that Paul's letter to the Romans is intended to show them the possibility of becoming the children of God rather than his slaves—the possibility of being sanctified. In Galatians, the phrase *form of God* must refer to the substance or essence of God. According to that reading, Philippians 2:6–7 can be paraphrased as follows: "Who, already being God, did not think to cling to his equality with God, but emptied himself and took upon himself the essence of a slave to be born as a mere human being." Two points can be made. First, if by becoming a human being Christ became a slave, then for Paul, to be a human is to be a slave. Whether we acknowledge our slavery or not, we are God's slaves: he owns us and we owe him. Thus, another way to see the question of Paul's letter to the Romans is to ask ourselves, Do we recognize him to whom we belong? As Leviticus 25:55 makes clear, the word *slave* describes not only the leaders of Israel, but also all Israelites. To be created by God is to belong to him. To enter into a covenant relationship with God is to recognize that we are his, to acknowledge that he is our master. We may recognize and acknowledge our true master, or we may rebel and pretend to choose another master, Satan.[29] (Lehi teaches something similar in 2 Nephi 2; see, for example, verse 27.) To repent and covenant is to return to our real owner and to recognize him as our Lord and Master. The second point is a rhetorical one. The Savior has himself become a slave, so Paul's reference to himself as a slave creates a parallel: as Christ is to the Father, so is Paul to Christ.

The fact that in taking human flesh on himself the Savior remained essentially God yet also became essentially a slave suggests a connection between Romans 1:1 and Moses 1:39: "For behold, this is my work and my glory—to bring to pass the immortality and eternal life of man." To be God is to be defined by the work, service, even servitude of a god. Thus, to be called as a slave to the Divine

is, in the end, to be called to be divine. It is to be called to be holy, sanctified, though the service one performs as a slave cannot itself make one divine. No amount of work a slave does can put the slave in position to inherit the estate of his master. Similarly, our service to God does not make us his children, though we can become his children.

Jesus Christ

Paul does not think of the word *Christ* as a name. The Savior's name is Jesus. The word *Christ* is a title, as the word order in verse 1 indicates. The phrase *Jesus the Christ* makes that quite clear.

The Greek word *christos* (χριστός), transliterated into English as "Christ," means "the anointed one." It is equivalent in meaning to the Hebrew word *messiah*. Israelite kings were anointed by the Lord through the prophet (see, for example, 1 Samuel 9:16; 10:1; 15:1, 17; 16:3, 12–13; 2 Samuel 12:7; Psalm 89:20; 1 Kings 19:15–16; 2 Kings 9:3, 6, 12; 2 Chronicles 22:7.) To be anointed king by the Lord is to be authorized by him to act. Perhaps more importantly, to be king is to become the representative of the people before the Lord. Considering both the authority denoted by anointing and the fact that the one anointed represents his people before God, no Christian can fail to see the significance of calling Jesus the Anointed One.

In addition to the king, the high priest was also anointed (for examples, see Leviticus 4:3, 5, 16; 1 Chronicles 29:22; Daniel 9:24). It is clear that the high priest's anointing denoted separation, consecration, sanctification, and cleansing, as well as authority. The high priest was considered the lawful successor of the Davidic king after the Babylonian exile.[30] Though kingship and priesthood functioned separately in Israel, the connection between them is obviously a part of Old Testament

> Paul, a servant of Jesus Christ, called to be an apostle, separated unto the gospel of God,

understanding. It thus becomes especially apropos to speak of Christ, who is both King and High Priest, as being anointed.[31]

Called

The King James translation, which reads "called to be an," is misleading. In the Greek, *called* is ambiguous. It may mean what the KJV says it does, but it can also be translated as an adjective modifying *apostle*. The latter possibility seems more likely.[32] The word *apostle* means literally "one sent out," in other words, a messenger. *Called* describes what kind of messenger Paul is. He is not just any messenger and especially not a self-appointed one; he is a called messenger. Unlike other messengers, Paul is a messenger because of his calling. Paul's language emphasizes his calling to the apostleship (compare Acts 9:1–21). His letter to the Galatians begins in a similar manner as Romans 1:1 does (see Galatians 1:1), perhaps because some doubted the authenticity of his calling (Acts 9:21 supports such a supposition).

Paul uses *called* several times in the opening of the letter to the Romans: in verse 1; in verse 6, where he speaks of the saints as those called by the name of Christ; and in verse 7, where he speaks of them as "called saints," again using *called* as an adjective. Paul's use of the word *called* implicitly compares the calling of the apostle and that of the saint. He is called as an apostle while we are called as saints. The life of a saint, and therefore the life of an apostle, is the appropriate response to the call of the gospel (see the discussion of the word *saints* in verse 7, pages 34–36). One of our callings is to be a saint, and Paul has par-

ticularly been called among the saints as an apostle, to be a messenger by and for Christ.

Paul may also be playing on the Greek word *klētos* (κλήτος), translated "called." If we compare the writings of John to those of Paul (though John wrote some time after Paul), we may see a play on the word *paraklētos* (παράκλητος), *paraclete* in English, meaning "the comforter." Literally, the word *paraclete* means "one who is called to be with another." A paraclete—a comforter—is a restorer, a mediator, a helper, a counselor, a defense, an advocate, a convincer, and a persuader. In John 14:16 the Savior speaks of both himself and the Holy Ghost as paracletes. Even if Paul is not playing on the connection of the word *klētos* to *paraklētos*, the gospel he has been called to preach proclaims that there is one who has been called to stand at our side, as a paraclete. As we will see (verse 12, pages 47–48), and as is incumbent on one called to be an apostle, Paul will also stand beside the saints as their paraclete. (In verse 12 a variation of *paraklētos* and, perhaps, of *klētos*, [called] is translated "comforted together.")

An apostle

As mentioned, the Greek word for *apostle* (*apostolos*, ἀπόστολος), means "one who has been sent" or "a messenger." The Hebrew and Aramaic terms to which this Greek word corresponds mean not just "messenger," but "authorized agent," particularly of a monarch. In the Greek translation of the Old Testament (known as the Septuagint; see page 4 and the discussion of verse 17, pages 65–66, for more on the Septuagint), *apostle* is used to mean not only a royal messenger, but a messenger with a special mission, as in Isaiah 6:8. In the Gospel of John, Jesus frequently uses the verb form of the Greek word (*apostellō*, ἀποστέλλω) to speak of himself as one sent from God (see John 3:17; 5:36, 38; 6:29, 57; 7:29; 8:42; 10:36; 11:42; 17:3, 8, 18, 21, 23, 25; 20:21). Paul uses the word *apostle* to emphasize his authority as a slave of God and to remind those who hear his letter of his divine calling and office.

A comparison of this verse to Romans 16:7 shows that the Greek word *apostolos* was a title in the early Christian church, not just a description of Paul's relation to his hearers. On the other hand, because that title was still new, people of Paul's time would have understood its ordinary Greek meaning, "messenger," at the same time that they understood it as a title. The word would have been meaningful in its own right in addition to being an official title.

Paul begins his letter by emphasizing that he has been called and that he is a messenger to the Romans. He has been sent from Jesus Christ to the world by being called, just as we become emissaries of Christ when we are called to serve in the kingdom. We take on ourselves the responsibility to fulfill our callings as one sent by the Lord.

One of the ironies of describing Paul as an apostle is that *apostolos* is a good translation of the Hebrew word *shaliyha* (שָׁלִיהַ), the title used for persons who were official representatives of the Sanhedrin court. Such representatives took documents with them to show they had legal authority in outlying synagogues.[33] Paul was serving as such a shaliyha, or apostolos, of the Jewish court—perhaps a constable in our terms—when he was on his way to Damascus to set in order the Jewish congregations there by persecuting the Christians. In other words, he was acting as an apostolos of the Sanhedrin when he was called to be an apostolos for the Lord. (The Greek word *apostolos* may have been used

among Christians as a translation of the Hebrew word *shaliyha*.)

Separated unto the gospel of God

Before considering the phrase *separated unto the gospel of God* as a whole, let us think about the word *separated*. Paul has not only been sent, but in being sent he has been separated, set apart, or appointed. He has been set apart to the gospel (see the discussion of *gospel*, pages 13–14.) In the New Testament the word used in verse 1, *aphorizō*, (ἀφορίζω) has two uses: with one exception (see Galatians 1:15) it refers to either the separation of the good from the wicked or supposedly wicked (see Matthew 13:49; 25:32; Luke 6:22; 2 Corinthians 6:17; Galatians 2:12) or the setting apart of someone for divine service (see Acts 13:2; 19:9). That the same word is used for separation from the wicked and for setting apart is surely no accident. Those set apart are to be different from—separate from—the wicked.

Aphorizō could also be translated "excommunicated." Perhaps Paul has been formally excommunicated from the synagogue by the rabbinical authorities. Given his change from one of the Sanhedrin's supporters in persecuting the Christians to a leader of the Christians, that would not be surprising. But even if Paul has not been excommunicated from the synagogue, he is no longer close to the hierarchy of Jewish ecclesiastical authority as he once was; he has been separated from them. One might suspect he has been separated from many of his friends as well, perhaps even from his family.

There is an important irony in the word *separated*: the word *Pharisee* probably means "separatist."[34] The Pharisees thought of themselves as those who had been separated or chosen. That is the origin of what, when it grew excessive, became a refusal to mingle

> Paul, a servant of Jesus Christ, called to be an apostle, separated unto the gospel of God,

with sinners and a denial of divine love (see, for example, Luke 15:1–2, the motivation for what we usually call the parable of the prodigal son). Like many early converts (see Acts 15:1–5), Paul is a former Pharisee (see Philippians 3:5). However, Paul has been separated from the separatists by—and to—the gospel of Jesus Christ.

The word *separated* may also imply more, though whether it does is arguable. The Old Testament directs that "when either man or woman shall separate themselves to vow a vow of a Nazarite, to separate themselves unto the Lord" (Numbers 6:2). Amos 2:11 indicates that Nazarites could be not only those who took a vow, but also those called of God to be Nazarites, as were both Samson and Samuel. A Nazarite is one who is consecrated to God, a person separated from the profane (ordinary) things of life for God's purposes, whether by his own vow or by God's calling. A Nazarite refrains from wine and any other grape products, neither cuts his hair nor shaves, and stays away from any contact with the dead because that would make him ritually impure (see Numbers 6:3–8).[35] Though Paul does not say he is a Nazarite, he speaks in terms appropriate for a Nazarite, and we know that he took Nazarite vows (see Acts 18:18 and perhaps 21:23–24), once perhaps about the time of this letter. The idea of being a Nazarite or of understanding a calling from God in terms analogous to the separation of the Nazarite could not be far from any Jewish writer's mind when using the Greek word here translated "separated." As a Jewish writer and especially under the circumstances, Paul almost certainly has this in mind.

Notice that whereas we speak of someone being cut off *from* a church or other group,

Paul says he has been cut off *to* the gospel. He has been separated from unrighteousness to the gospel. Similarly, if we will be members of Christ's church, we must be separated from ungodliness; we must be excommunicated—separated—from the world to the gospel.

We use the phrase *set apart* much as Paul uses *separated*. We are accustomed to the phrase *set apart*, or we grow accustomed to it after our conversion to the church. Consequently, unless we are among those who have grown up as something other than Latter-day Saints and are still young enough in the church to be not yet accustomed to the phrase, we probably do not see that *set apart to* is as odd a term as *separated*. It is also equally meaningful. Notice that Acts 13:2 says that Paul and Barnabas were "separated for" the preaching of the gospel in Antioch. Today we would say they were "set apart." Thinking about what the New Testament means when it says that people are separated for a calling and about the word's connection to the vow of a Nazarite may add depth to our understanding of the things to which we have been set apart.

The entire phrase *separated unto the gospel of God*, like the two phrases before it (*a servant of Jesus Christ* and *called to be an apostle*), is an appositive to *Paul*. Each describes Paul. As a result of his calling, Paul has been separated, or set apart, to the gospel. He has been separated from his past life to the church in order to preach the gospel. Paul has also been separated within the community of the church as a messenger of Christ, as an apostle.

According to Greek thinking, a thing is what it is because of the way in which it is distinct from other things. Something is defined, therefore, by that which distinguishes it, that which separates it from other things.[36] This Greek idea can be used well in consonance with the Hebrew and Christian idea that to be set apart, or separated unto, is to be made into a new person by being given a new relation to the rest of existence. Paul is who he is because a line has been drawn between him and everything else. Paul's calling to preach the gospel has separated him from everything both within and without the church; his calling has given him his definition, or being.

Gospel

The Greek word *euangelion* (ἐυαγγέλιον) literally means "good news," "pleasing message," or even simply "goodness." In the Septuagint the word is used seven times to mean "good news" (see 2 Samuel 18:20, 22, 25, 27; 2 Kings 7:9). The word is used to announce such things as the birth of an heir to the throne,[37] and New Testament writers used the term as an implicit expansion of that usage. Additionally, the Greek word originally referred to the reward a messenger received for bringing good news, and there seems still to be something of this implied in the New Testament usage. (Compare this use of the word *euangelion* to the Septuagint's use of it in 2 Samuel 4:10 and 18:22, where it means "a reward for good news.")

The New Testament use of the word *gospel* is heavily influenced by the Old Testament use of the Hebrew word *basar* (בשׂר) translated "good tidings," "tidings," and "publish" in verses such as 1 Samuel 31:9; 1 Kings 1:42; and Jeremiah 20:15. In the Septuagint, the basic meaning of the verb from which *euangelion* is derived is "to announce news," especially news of victory and, by extension, the advent of salvation, the victory over spiritual and physical death. "News of victory" is the meaning of *euangelion* in such verses as Psalms 40:10 and 96:3 ("declare" in the KJV); Isaiah 40:9; 41:27; 52:7; 61:1 (where the KJV has "good tidings"); 60:6 ("praises"); and

Nahum 1:15 ("good tidings"). Given the meaning of the Greek word *euangelion* and the fact that the Greek usage in the New Testament reflects the Old Testament's concepts, we can see that the word *gospel* refers to the proclamation of an event, the victory over both physical and spiritual death announced by the coming of the Heavenly King.

The content of that announcement is essential, but it cannot be reduced to a matter of dogmatic concern. The prophets of the Old Testament demanded that Israel listen, and they equated hearing with obeying: "Hear, O Israel: The Lord our God is one Lord."[38] New Testament writers consider the preaching of the gospel similarly. They announce the news that the Divine King has come, and they expect those to whom they preach to hear. They expect the response "Hosanna, blessed is he who comes in the name of the Lord."[39]

We often think of the gospel as the beliefs, doctrines, and so on, that are taught by the Church of Jesus Christ of Latter-day Saints. Sometimes we use the word *gospel* even more broadly, to refer to Christianity and the Christian message generally. However, the New Testament use of the word *gospel* is tied more closely to its literal meaning (pleasing message) and to its Old Testament connections. Just as Christ's redemption is the act of redeeming us rather than the doctrinal meaning of that redemption, the gospel is for New Testament writers primarily the proclamation of that redemption, the preaching and the hearing of the pleasing message.[40] The doctrinal content of the gospel is important but still secondary to the life and preaching of the gospel.[41] Thus when Paul says he has been separated to the gospel, he means he has been set apart to preach the good news of Christ's life, redemption, and resurrection.

The close connection of the word *gospel* (*euangelion*, ἐυαγγέλιον), meaning "pleasing

> (Which he had promised afore by his prophets in the holy scriptures,)

message," with Paul's calling as an apostle (literally, a messenger) can hardly be accidental. The word *called* and words meaning "messenger" and "pleasing message," each associated with the voice and the use of the voice, occur almost right next to each other in verse 1, demanding that we hear the message Paul has been called to give. (After all, originally this letter was probably intended to be read aloud to the congregation rather than circulated and read as we would read a book of scripture.) Throughout the scriptures we see this connection between the preaching of the gospel message and conversion. Enos, for example, says that remembering the words his father spoke moved him to prayer and, according to one reading of Enos 1:5, to sanctification (see Enos 1:1–5, especially verse 3). Alma also tells us of the power of preaching: "The preaching of the word had a great tendency to lead the people to do that which was just—yea, it had had more powerful effect upon the minds of the people than the sword, or anything else" (Alma 31:5). The scriptures teach us the importance of knowledge (though not necessarily just any knowledge).[42] As important as knowledge is, however, preaching and listening to the gospel are more important in that preaching and listening bring us to do what the Lord requires, and simple knowledge may not.[43]

In verses 2–4, Paul defines the pleasing message, or gospel, he has been set apart to deliver: it is the pleasing message of salvation that has Jesus Christ as both its author and its content.

The gospel of God

There are two ways to read the word *of* in the phrase *the gospel of God*. According to one

reading, the phrase means "the good news about God." According to the other it means "the good news from God." As Fitzmyer argues, the second is more likely.[44] Paul clarifies that the good news about Jesus Christ's sacrifice comes from the Father: God's good news is the news of his Son. Thus Paul's preaching focuses on teaching us to understand our relation to the Son.

Joseph Smith Translation (JST) Verse 1

> Paul, <u>an apostle, a servant of God, called of Jesus Christ, and separated to preach the gospel,</u>[45]

The Prophet Joseph's version of verse 1 emphasizes Paul's call by rearranging the verse. This arrangement makes it more clear that Paul is asserting his authority. As we saw earlier, the Greek text uses three phrases appositive to *Paul*, each one equal to the other: *a servant, a called apostle,* and *one separated to the gospel.* The King James translation does not make clear the equivalence of these three phrases, seeming to emphasize *a servant* and allowing us to read *separated unto the gospel of God* as an appositive to *called to be an apostle.* The Joseph Smith Translation divides the three descriptions of Paul into four and rearranges them: Paul is "an apostle" and he is "a servant of God." These two noun phrases are parallel, and they are followed by two more parallel phrases, *called of Jesus Christ* and *separated to preach the gospel.* These two parallels are themselves parallel in that *called of Jesus Christ* can be understood to explain what it means to be "an apostle," and *separated to preach the gospel* can be understood to explain what it means to be "a servant of God."

Both the King James and the Joseph Smith versions finish the verse with two passive verb phrases that use the same two passive verbs (*called* and *separated*). However, the King James Version tells us that Paul has been called to be an apostle and separated to the gospel, while the Joseph Smith version tells us that Paul has been called by Jesus Christ and separated for preaching. In the Joseph Smith revision, the phrase *called of Jesus Christ* focuses on Paul's experience on the road to Damascus, the miraculous event in which he was called to be the authoritative messenger he is. Like the first two descriptive phrases in the JST (*an apostle* and *a servant*), this phrase emphasizes Paul's authority by shifting the emphasis from Paul's servitude to the authority of his calling.

The second of these two passive verb phrases, *separated to preach the gospel*, brings the preaching of the gospel to the fore, something that is evident in the Greek but missing in the King James translation.

Verse 2

Verse 2 is the first verse in a five-verse parenthetical statement. Verse 1 tells whom the letter is from, and verse 7 tells whom it is to. As mentioned earlier, this is a fairly standard, though expanded, beginning for a letter of the time. In verses 2–6, however, is something that probably would have surprised Paul's audience or at least struck them as odd: a digression in the middle of the salutation. In this digression Paul explains his gospel preaching and how the gospel came about through Jesus Christ.

A digression of this length at this particular point is an oddity in a letter of Paul's time, but digressions in general were not unusual. Though such long digressions from the theme may impede our understanding today, many Greek writers and thinkers considered them good style. Brevity was not necessarily a virtue. The audience who first heard this letter read was sufficiently accustomed to these digressions to understand what was being said. Digressions, however, may take some work for us to get used to.

One reason that Paul's contemporaries could keep track of digressions better than we can today is that the connectives in Greek—the words used to link sentences and phrases together—were more meaningful to them than English connectives are to us. Spoken, not written, language was the standard, both because many could not read and because the lack of a printing press made the widespread distribution of written material impossible. Greek speakers used rhetorical and grammatical conventions to connect their ideas effectively; such conventions were a kind of oral punctuation. Written Greek had no punctuation marks to show where sentences ended and how clauses related to each other, because such marks were, strictly speaking, unnecessary. The grammatical forms of the nouns and verbs kept sentences separate, as they do for us, but connectives—words like *and*, *but*, *furthermore*, and so on—clarified relations between clauses. Greek speakers often used these connectives between sentences to show the relation of the sentences to each other. (Sometimes they were used as pauses between sentences, much as we often use *uh* or *you know* in ordinary speech.) By paying attention to connectives, people who spoke Greek (the common language of the civilized world in Paul's time) avoided being confused by digressions.[46]

A similar, frequent use of connectives is apparent in the language of the Book of Mormon, in which the writers often begin passages and even several successive sentences with *and it came to pass*. The function of such connectives in the Book of Mormon seems to have been different from their function in Greek, but the two languages are like each other and different from English in that good

> (Which he had promised afore by his prophets in the holy scriptures,)

writers of both languages use connectives frequently, while good writers of English do not.

Although digressions have generally been considered poor style since the end of the nineteenth century—they are typically relegated to footnotes or left out altogether—they are more than a cultural artifact. In both speech and writing, digressions serve a useful function. Ancient writers used them because they can add depth that cannot be achieved in simple, declarative sentences. Because scientific writing requires simplicity and getting right to the point, and because in the eighteenth and nineteenth centuries physical science became the model of all knowledge for us, we prize simplicity and getting to the point.[47] Ancient speakers and writers prized thoroughness. Digressions allowed them to show various facets of the subject matter or other ideas the subject matter reminded them of, and digressions allowed writers to show how all these things are interconnected. Without digressions, Greek writers often found it difficult to show the fullness and depth of the gospel. Thus a Greek writer like Paul or a Hebrew writer like Isaiah might have thought that simple sentences, speeches, and letters or essays with only one real point oversimplified the truth, while complexity, including the complexity created by digressions, allowed a writer to be more true to the richness of the subject matter. The Greek language allowed writers to be complex and use digressions without getting lost. Paul likely used digressions, as well as various rhetorical and grammatical patterns, to show how rich any gospel topic is.

Promised

The Greek word translated "promised" (*proepangellō*, προεπαγγέλλω) is etymologically related to the Greek word translated "gospel" (*euangelion*): they share a root meaning, "to announce" (*angellō*, ἀγγέλλω). The apostle is the messenger, the announcer, of the promise. This conceptual connection of *apostle* to *gospel* and *promised* also suggests that *apostle* is connected to *angel*. The word *angel* is also etymologically related to the words translated "gospel" and "promised," and like the word for *apostle*, the Greek word translated "angel" (*angelos*, ἄγγελος) means "announcer" or "messenger." Paul's message is that the promises made anciently through the prophets have been fulfilled.

Prophets

The Greek word *prophētēs* (προφήτης), obviously a cognate of the word *prophet*, means "an interpreter," one who speaks for another, one who explains what another is saying. The prophets speak to us for God, interpreting his will for us. The Old Testament contains the gospel, the good news of Jesus Christ, because the Old Testament prophets preach of Christ. If the Old Testament preached something other than Jesus Christ, then God would have changed his message from the Old Testament to the New Testament, because the gospel of Jesus Christ certainly is taught in the New Testament. That the gospel is the message of the Old Testament may not be readily apparent to those who read it without a knowledge of Christ. However, those who do know of him can see his gospel in it. Given what we have seen in verse 1, namely, Paul's emphasis on his calling as a messenger of God, Paul is surely implicitly identifying himself with the ancient prophets and his message of Christ with theirs.

Holy scriptures

Romans 1:2 is the only place in the New Testament where this particular Greek phrase translated "holy scriptures" can be found

(2 Timothy 3:15 KJV uses the phrase *holy scriptures*, but it translates from a different Greek phrase than the one we find here). For Paul, the scriptures are essentially what we refer to as the Old Testament. Modern Jews divide the Old Testament into the Law, the Writings, and the Prophets, and they presumably also divided it that way in Paul's time. However, the notion of a scriptural canon was not as rigorous in Paul's time as it is today. As we will see from the ways in which Paul refers to the Wisdom of Solomon—Wisdom, for short—Paul uses some books as scripture that modern Christians do not presently use as scripture.[48] Paul seems to implicitly refer to or paraphrase Wisdom in the following references: Romans 1:19–23 (compare Wisdom 13:1–19; 14:22–31); 1:26 (compare Wisdom 11:15–16; 12:27); 1:29–32 (compare Wisdom 14:23–26); 2:4 (compare Wisdom 15:1–3); 5:12 (compare Wisdom 2:24); and 5:14 (compare Wisdom 1:14).

Which he had promised afore by his prophets in the holy scriptures

By using the phrase *which he had promised afore by his prophets in the holy scriptures*, Paul indicates he is not doing something new; the gospel he preaches was preached anciently and is available in the scriptures. Paul's calling is to preach the gospel, to announce that Jesus is the Christ and that redemption comes through faith in him. However, Paul is not the only source of that message, nor are the others who have been called as apostles. The gospel message has already been promised to those who will read the scriptures with understanding. Part of the message of every prophet is that what he preaches is not new but was promised from the beginning. Though new to those who repent (when they were unrepentant they could not hear it), the gospel is everlasting, for it has been preached from the beginning and will always be true. It is both new and everlasting.

While the gospel is not new because it has always existed, Paul, like any other Christian apostle, is definitely introducing something new to the Jews, namely, a new way of understanding and reading the material that we call the Old Testament. Paul is introducing something that will separate Christians from Jews for millennia to come: the question of how to interpret the Old Testament. Along with other Christians, Paul says that the Old Testament, the old covenant, promises the gospel he preaches, which is the new covenant recorded in the writings that are now called the New Testament. Jews did not then and do not now agree that the New Testament is a fulfillment of the Old. One way to highlight the difference between Christians and Jews is to ask whether the books of the Law, the Writings, and the Prophets (the three traditional Jewish divisions of their scriptures, our Old Testament) testify of Christ. If they do, then they are a testament that has been available from ancient times. They are an old testament, and the records of Matthew, Mark, Luke, John, Paul, and others are a new testament, a second witness for the divinity of Christ. The difference between other Christians and Mormons can be similarly highlighted by asking whether the Book of Mormon is a third testament of Christ's divinity. Of course, Mormons believe it is, and the subtitle that was recently added, "Another Testament of Jesus Christ," is as appropriate as the names Old Testament and New Testament are.

JST Verse 2

(Which he had promised <u>before</u> by his prophets in the holy scriptures,)

The only difference between the King James Version and the Joseph Smith Translation is the change of *afore* to *before*, a minor change. Presumably the Prophet was modernizing the language with this change.

> Concerning his Son Jesus Christ our Lord,
> which was made of the seed of David accord-
> ing to the flesh;

Verse 3

Following Rudolf Bultmann, many scholars believe that Romans 1:3–4 uses the language of an already existing formula of confession, something like a short version of our
Articles of Faith.[49] These two verses together
give us Paul's definition of the gospel. It is
the news that Jesus, a descendent of David
the king, was resurrected and declared by
God to be his holy Son.

Concerning his Son Jesus Christ our Lord

Jesus Christ is the content of the message
of the gospel. It is what Paul as well as the
previous prophets has taught. In the phrase
concerning his Son Jesus Christ our Lord we see
the bone of contention between Jews and
Christians: is Jesus the Anointed One, and
does the Old Testament prophesy of him?
This debate exists not only between Christians and Jews, but among fellow Christians.
In the eighteenth century, Christian scholars
took up the question of whether the Old Testament prophesies of Jesus, and that debate
continues today. Many Christian scholars
now believe that to read the Old Testament as
prophesying of Christ is to read things into
the material of the Old Testament. Obviously,
Paul does not share that understanding.

Son

The Greek word translated "son" (*huios*,
υἱός), is a familial term, just as is the English
word *son*. It implies a father and a mother. It
can also be translated more generally as "off-
spring," "heir," or "descendent." In any case,
the term clearly implies a familial, genetic relation. Of course, the use of such a term does

not of itself establish the correctness of the
Latter-day Saint understanding of Jesus' sonship. It is possible to use the term metaphorically. However, we who believe that Jesus is
the literal Son of God are reminded of that belief here.

Cranfield points out that the construction
of verses 3 and 4 suggests that Jesus was the
Son before his earthly birth.[50] Paul teaches
that Jesus did not become the Son of God
through his ministry. It was not an earthly
achievement, but a status that he held even
before his birth as the literal Son of God.[51]

Lord

Palestinian Jews called Yahweh *Lord*. By
using the word *Lord* to refer to Jesus, Paul explicitly identifies Jesus with Yahweh.[52] As
Peter recognizes, that identification is a scandal to the Jews (see 1 Peter 2:8). This is the
lord, the master, whom Paul serves as a slave.
Paul is implicitly comparing his calling to
that of the Old Testament prophets.

His Son Jesus Christ our Lord

The possessive pronouns *his* and *our* in
the phrase *his Son Jesus Christ our Lord* show
the parallel between Jesus as the Son of God
and Jesus as our Lord, as well as identify the
emphasis of the phrase. They remind us that
Jesus is the Son of God and is thus our Lord,
literally "our master." Jesus is the Son, not a
slave (at least not in this context), but we are
slaves. We are not yet God's children, in spite
of the fact that we are his literal spiritual off-
spring; we gave up our birthright as his spiritual children when we sinned. As things currently stand, we are not yet the Father's, but
as converts to Christ we are slaves of the
Father's Son (see the discussion of *servant* in
verse 1, pages 3–9). By speaking of the Son as
our owner and master, Paul draws our attention to the problem to which the gospel is an

answer, namely, the relationship of divinity to humanity. There seems to be an absolute gap between God and humanity, between the sinful and the sinless, a gap that makes returning to the Father—being related to him in the way that Jesus is related to him—seem impossible. This is the problem for humans, the problem that Paul addresses in this letter by preaching the gospel.

Most religions recognize this gap between divinity and humanity, but Christianity is unique in seeing a bridge across that gap. Greek culture and Christianity both agree that our inability to bridge the gap is the substance of tragedy. The Greek tragedians explored the tragedy of separation from divinity with nuance and sophistication. There may be no better investigations of what it means to be merely human than the Greek tragedies, and the only meaning those tragedies show is suffering. To be human is to suffer, sometimes because of what we do, sometimes for no apparent reason. Christians also recognize that to be human is to suffer, and this suffering is not always, perhaps not even mostly, because of what we have done. But Christianity goes beyond that recognition. It responds to the tragedy of human existence by showing a way across the gap between the divine and the human. The gap is not crossed by the human becoming divine, but by the divine becoming human. According to Latter-day Saint theology, this is what makes it possible for the human to become divine.[53] Thus when philosophy seeks to understand human suffering in the context of theodicy (the problem of how a perfect, all-loving, and all-powerful God could allow suffering), it has already misunderstood Christianity. The gospel is not an answer to the problem of suffering, nor a resolution, nor even a dissolution of it. The gospel is a *response* to suffering. It is the announcement that God has joined with us in

our suffering (see Hebrews 5:8; D&C 122). He has condescended to become like us, and because he has, he can offer us salvation. He does not offer a surcease of suffering in this life, but he can give us strength, a lightening of our burden (see Matthew 11:28–30), and the promise of salvation.

According to

The Greek word translated "according to" indicates purpose, fitness, or relation. In this case, the last of these seems the only possibility: "in relation to the flesh."

Flesh

Paul sometimes uses *flesh* as a negative term (see, for example, Romans 8:3), but it is apparent in verse 3 that he does not always do so. He also uses *flesh* to represent the body (see verse 3), and I think he sometimes also uses it to refer to the redeemed human being (see Galatians 2:20). Scriptural terms are almost never unequivocal. Our desire to read them as if they were is, as much as anything else, a sign of the influence of the philosophies of our time, a time in which univocity and simplicity, the marks of legalism and scientific thinking, are considered more intellectually rigorous and fruitful than richness and depth. (See the comments on digression in the discussion of verse 2, pages 15–16. Similar comments apply here.) We cannot simply equate *flesh* with *sin* or any other negative term. When Paul does use *flesh* negatively, it is always in contrast to the spirit, a contrast Paul makes much of as he discusses the spirit and the law, grace, and works. We should remember, however, that he begins this letter not only by noticing the contrast of the spirit and the flesh, but what is more important, by pointing out that the same supposed contrast is found in Christ. Thus though the spirit and the flesh may be opposed to one another at

> And declared to be the Son of God with power, according to the spirit of holiness, by the resurrection from the dead:

times, the Savior's life shows that they do not have to be. Not only are they not opposed in the resurrected Christ (an image Paul uses in Romans 4 to illustrate the relation between faith and works), but they are also not in opposition in the mortal Jesus. Christ's life on the earth—in the flesh—is a promise that we can overcome what seems a necessary and inescapable opposition. The gap between the divine and the human cannot be reduced to the difference between spirit and flesh. Our bodies, our mortality, can be redeemed (see Romans 8:23). Thus the contrast of flesh and spirit is a model for what life "in the Spirit" (Romans 8:9) means as well as the source for Paul's discussion of life without the Spirit. (The two ways of understanding flesh and spirit are developed more fully in Romans 7 and 8.)

Latter-day revelation adds an interesting insight to this contrast of spirit and flesh. The soul is said to be the unity of the spirit and the body (see D&C 88:15). The life of sin, the life in which spirit and body are at odds, is thus a life in which the soul is alienated from and at odds with itself. Christ's redemption is a promise that the alienation of spirit and body can be overcome not, as some would sometimes have it, by the negation of the body but by the perfect unity of both body and spirit. The atonement is not only a reconciliation of the human and the divine, it makes possible the reconciliation of a person with him- or herself, the reconciliation of flesh and spirit.

Note that because Paul uses this contrast between flesh and spirit without comment, he must assume that it is a contrast his audience is familiar with. Contrary to what one some-

times hears about New Testament doctrine, the contrast of flesh and spirit was not invented by Paul.

Made

The Greek verb translated "made" (*gignomai*, γίγνομαι) seems to have originally referred to birth,[54] as it does here, even though by Paul's time it was not usually used to denote birth (compare Galatians 4:4, where the same Greek word is used). Cranfield has suggested that this may be Paul's way of recognizing the virgin birth.[55]

David

Compare 2 Timothy 2:8, as well as Hebrews 7:14 and the genealogies of the Savior given in Matthew and Luke (see Matthew 1:1–17; Luke 3:23–38). Christ is a king by earthly as well as heavenly right. However, Mark 12:35–37 suggests that during Jesus' lifetime, many were not aware that the Messiah would be a descendent of David. If they had known that doctrine, the riddle Jesus proposes in Mark 12 might not have been a riddle.

Made of the seed of David according to the flesh

Jesus is David's heir. As such he is the king of Israel in both the flesh and the spirit. In the phrase *made of the seed of David according to the flesh* we see how flesh and spirit come together in the gospel in the person of Christ.

JST Verse 3

No change.

Verse 4

Verse 4 is a short synopsis of the pleasing message that Paul conveys: Christ, the Son of God, has power and has been resurrected, initiating the resurrection of all.

Declared

The Greek word translated "declared" (*horizō*, ὁρίζω) means "to mark out" or "to set bounds." It is the origin of our word *horizon*. In the New Testament, *horizō* is always used to mean "define," "determine," or "appoint" (see Luke 22:22; Acts 2:23; 10:42; 11:29; 17:26, 31; Hebrews 4:7). The word is the root of *aphorizō*, translated "separated" in verse 1 and "predestinate" in Romans 8:29. Taken literally, *set apart* means much the same thing as does *horizō*, or *declared*.

If, by paying attention to the Greek, we understand *declared* to mean "to mark out," "define," or "determine," Jesus is defined as the Son of God by his resurrection from the dead. That event marks him out, separates him, from anyone else. New Testament writers sometimes use the resurrection as the symbol for the atonement (see, for example, John 11:25; Acts 1:22; Philippians 3:10–11; 1 Peter 1:3). Paul especially does this. Because as Latter-day Saints we make important technical distinctions between such things as salvation and exaltation, we sometimes misunderstand the New Testament way of speaking, imputing our distinctions to writings where those distinctions are not made. For New Testament writers, the resurrection is a symbol of the atonement, perhaps even *the* symbol of the atonement because it brings the spirit and the flesh together for eternity. In keeping with the implicit discussion of how Christ unifies the physical and the spiritual, Paul emphasizes that because of the redemption we can be made alive again, both spiritually and physically. The parts of our lives that seem at odds with each other, for example, our spirits and our bodies, can be made whole. The war in the flesh between the various aspects of our character (see Romans 7:8–23) is brought to an end through the resurrection, which is a type and symbol on the

one hand and a literal fact on the other. Thus the resurrection is an apt symbol of Christ's redemptive sacrifice. In verse 4 we see Paul saying that Jesus of Nazareth is the Son of God, not by virtue of qualities he has but by virtue of his saving act. That he overcame both physical and spiritual death makes him the Son of God. Our Heavenly Father gave us spiritual birth, but we gave up that spiritual inheritance to come to the earth as embodied beings. The Son gave us back that spiritual inheritance; he made our rebirth, our adoption, possible. By imitating the Father in giving us spiritual birth, Jesus is the Son of the Father. Because he gives us birth, however, he also becomes our Father. (I take it that the first several verses of Mosiah 15 say something like this.)

As noted above, *horizō* is the root of *aphorizō*, translated "separated" in verse 1. Paul seems to be making a play on words, using the relation between these two words to draw a connection we might not otherwise see: Paul's call to be an apostle is a type of Christ's call to be the Redeemer, just as Paul's divine service is a type of the Savior's sacrifice. (This may say something about what it means to take up our cross. See, for example, Matthew 16:24; Mark 8:34; 10:21; Luke 9:23; 3 Nephi 12:30; D&C 23:6; 56:2; 112:14. It suggests that to be called to serve is to be called to imitate the Savior in doing the will of the Father without self-aggrandizement.)

In discussing the phrase *separated unto the gospel of God* (verse 1), I pointed out that according to the Greek way of thinking, a thing is defined or determined by its delimitation from other things. The perfection of something is what makes it what it is rather than something else—the specific difference, to use the language of Aristotle.[56] Because we as Latter-day Saints are part of a twentieth-century culture, we tend to think of being perfect in

> And declared to be the Son of God with power, according to the spirit of holiness, by the resurrection from the dead:

terms of how perfection is conceived in the twentieth century rather than how it was conceived anciently; we think that to be perfect is to be without flaw. We also tend to think that a perfect being is able to exceed all bounds and limitations. In contrast, for ancient Greek thinkers and in the Greek language, a person or object is perfect by being circumscribed within a whole, by having definite boundaries that clearly distinguish it from other things. The perfect vase, for example, is the vase that most perfectly fits the definition, the boundaries set for vases. The boundaries of the vase, the elements of its definition, tell us what the perfect vase is. They distinguish it from every other thing and they show how it relates to each other thing, giving it its place in the world. Thus for someone like Paul, a Greek speaker in a predominantly Greek culture, the perfect thing is the thing that is in its assigned place and order. In this way of thinking, Christ's perfection is found in his appointment as the Son of God. He is perfect because he fulfills the measure set out by that declaration, by that marking of boundaries. Presumably, we can similarly understand what it means for us to be perfect: it is to fill the measure to which we have been appointed, whatever that measure is (and it may differ from person to person as well as from time to time).

This Greek understanding of perfection, an understanding Paul alludes to in verse 4, should make us reconsider at least some of what we say about scriptures such as Matthew 5:48: "Be ye therefore perfect, even as your Father which is in heaven is perfect." I believe that this scripture is a quotation of Leviticus 19:2 or at least a reference to it: "Ye shall be holy: for I the Lord your God am holy," and holiness is a major theme of this letter to the Romans. (For more about holiness, see the discussion of *saints* in the commentary on verse 7, pages 34–36.) It may even be that this letter is an interpretation of Leviticus 19 for the Roman saints. If so, still other ways to put the question of this letter are, What does it mean to be holy? and What does it mean to be sanctified?

Perhaps surprisingly, neither Leviticus 19:2 nor Matthew 5:48 is necessarily a commandment. In Hebrew and Greek, each is in the simple future tense: you will be holy; you will be perfect. In both languages, as in English, the simple future can be used to express a command (for example, "You *will* do the dishes"), or it can be a simple statement of fact (for example, "You will get cold if you don't wear a coat"). When written in verses such as these, the simple future is ambiguous: it may be a command or it may be a statement of what will be in the future.[57] I think we can take that ambiguity to indicate that the Lord's commandments are also statements of future facts: he will have a holy and perfect people.

If we consider this ambiguity seriously, we can read Leviticus and Matthew differently than we are accustomed to, but still profitably. (That different reading may also apply to 3 Nephi 12:48.) If we take Leviticus and Matthew to be expressing statements of future facts as well as commandments, then we see the Lord describing his people in those verses—not as they now are, but as they will be. According to this reading, Leviticus 19:2 and Matthew 5:48 are as much promises as they are commandments. (See Mosiah 4:12, which suggests that the subsequent "commandments" in verses 13–16 are as much blessings as commandments; and D&C 59:4, in which blessings, commandments, and revelations seem to be equated with one another.) Paul will address the question of how the saints are, as yet, unholy and imperfect. Eventually he will tell them how they can be holy and perfect. As the Lord does in Leviticus 19, Paul will show them how, though they have been converted and baptized, they are not yet the people of the Lord ("the children of Christ," to use King Benjamin's language [Mosiah 5:7]; "perfect," to use the language of Matthew). Paul will then show them what it means to be holy or perfect, in other words, how they can be made the children of Christ and the Father.

Though we cannot legitimately substitute the word *perfected* for the word *declared* in the phrase *declared to be the Son of God*, it is important to see the connection of this declaration to being perfected. It is as if Paul is saying, "And perfected (or perfectly defined) to be the Son of God." Christ is already perfect and, in so being, is already a child of God in the fullest sense, or scriptural sense. In spite of their divine heritage, those in Paul's audience are imperfect because of sin. They have yet to become children of Christ and, as such, children of God. The question is how that imperfection is to be overcome.

Though it is important to understand how the Greek word *horizō* (translated "declared"), is related to the word *aphorizō* (translated "separated") in verse 1, and though it is important to see what the word *horizō* may imply about perfection and the theme of the letter, it is also important to recognize that "declared" is a useful and informative translation. In raising Jesus from the dead, in bringing the flesh and the spirit together again, the Father *declared*—announced—Jesus to be his Son, the Christ. In addition, it is historically accurate to say that the resurrection itself *declared* Jesus to be the Son of God. To a real extent, many, including the apostles, did not understand who Christ was until the resurrection. Even the foremost apostle, Peter, seems not to have understood, in spite of the testimony he gave of Jesus' messiahship (see Matthew 16:13–20; 26:35, 69–75; Luke 24:12). For those in the ancient church and for us, Jesus' resurrection *declared* his relation to the Father. Finally, Christ's resurrection is a type of our redemption, physical as well as spiritual, that by which we will be *declared* to be the children of God.

The Son of God

Jesus' inheritance is dual. Not only is he David's heir and therefore Israel's rightful earthly king, but he is also, and most importantly, the Son of God, the spiritual king of Israel. The image of the physical and the spiritual coming together in Christ is continued in the phrase *the Son of God*. In Christ, the spirit and the body come together; in him, spiritual and earthly power are united. In Christ, these seeming dichotomies are no longer at odds with one another.

Throughout the letter, Paul plays with the idea of dichotomies. He often uses a word so that it entails its opposite. For example, he sometimes uses the word *death* to refer to our coming into life in Christ, in other words, to refer to spiritual life (see, for example, Romans 6:2–7). At other times he uses the same word to mean spiritual death (see, for example, Romans 1:32). Though we sometimes find his multivalent use of words confusing, he uses them because they allow him to illustrate the points he wants to make. Paul's point seems to be, among other things, that in the gospel the oppositions between life and death, spirit and flesh, peace and wrath, and so on, are overcome (see also the discussion of *resurrection*, page 26).

> And declared to be the Son of God with power, according to the spirit of holiness, by the resurrection from the dead:

With power

As the alternate translation indicates, "powerfully" or "in power" is probably a preferable translation to "with power." Like the English word *power*, the Greek word can indicate strength, might, power, and ability, and it is important to remember not only the first three of these, but the last one as well. Christ is the Son of God because of his ability, presumably the ability to carry out the will of the Father, the ability to save us. I think his might and power are best understood in terms of that ability to save, rather than the reverse.

In translating the phrase *with power*, one must ask what it modifies. We can read it as modifying either *declared* or *Son of God*. In the first case, Paul is saying that Jesus was declared to be the Son of God by a mighty act of God, namely, the resurrection. In the second case, Paul is saying that Christ has power, that he is a source of power. Both Fitzmyer and Cranfield prefer the second interpretation. For example, Fitzmyer argues that since the power in question is the power by which the Father brings about the resurrection and by which the Son gives life to human beings, it makes the most sense to understand *in power* as modifying *Son of God*.[58] I disagree. Of course one must grant that the Father and the Son have power. That is not in question. However, to read the power as the power of the Son rather than as the power of the event by which Jesus' sonship is announced seems odd. The topic under discussion is the appointment of Jesus as the Son of God rather than Jesus himself. To read *in power* as modi-

fying *declared* lends force to that topic. To read it as modifying *Son of God* is to take *in power* to be a digression. Because the first is a stronger reading than the second, I think the first fits the context better.

According to the spirit of holiness

In the phrase *according to the spirit of holiness* is the same Greek word translated "according to" in verse 3 (*kata*, κάτα). Paul is using the same word to make sure that his audience sees the parallel he is creating. In verse 4, there seems to be two ways to understand the phrase. One is to take this to mean that Christ was appointed to be the Son of God through the power of the spirit of holiness. The other is to take it to mean that his appointment is guaranteed by the spirit of holiness.

However, there is a problem in deciding which ideas the connective word translated "according to" joins. It is possible that it connects *spirit of holiness* to the word *declared*: "declared to be the Son of God according to the spirit of holiness." Or it may connect the word *power* to the phrase *spirit of holiness*: "powerfully, in other words, according to the spirit of holiness." Though the first case is possible, it is less likely than the second.

Spirit of holiness

One of Paul's themes is the connection of the spirit to holiness. Given that theme, it may be helpful to notice that the phrase *spirit of holiness* is a pleonasm (a redundancy), since what is truly of the spirit is holy.

It is not obvious here whether *spirit* (*pnuema*, πνεῦμα) refers particularly to the Holy Ghost. It may be a Greek translation of a Hebrew phrase that refers specifically to God and to any person whose spirit is holy as God is holy. (For Old Testament uses of the

Hebrew phrase—*ruach qadosh,* רוּחַ קֹדֶשׁ—see, for example, Psalm 51:11; Isaiah 63:10–11.) If this is the case, Paul uses the word *spirit* in contrast to flesh (as in verse 3). Christ is the son of David in terms of his flesh, and Christ is the Son of God in terms of his spirit, which is a holy spirit. The contrast of the spirit and the flesh is one of Paul's most important themes, and Paul introduces that contrast by reference to both the body and the spirit of Christ, in whom the two are not in conflict.

On the other hand, this phrase may refer to the Holy Ghost rather than to the personal spirit of the Savior. There are two problems with this interpretation, however. First, if this phrase is intended to refer to the Holy Ghost, then we would expect the wording to be different. We would expect the Greek equivalent of *Holy Ghost* rather than of *spirit of holiness.* The Greek phrase translated "Holy Ghost" is *pneuma hagion* (πνεῦμα ἅγιον), literally "Holy Spirit." Here, however, Paul uses *pneuma hagiōsunēs* (πνεῦμα ἁγιωσύνης), literally "spirit of holiness," as the King James translation has it. If this phrase refers to the Holy Ghost, this is the only case where that wording is used to do so. Nevertheless, Paul may be referring to the Holy Ghost, using the phrase *of holiness (hagiōsunēs)* rather than the word *holy (hagios)* to emphasize the purifying nature of the Holy Ghost's work. The second problem is that if we understand this phrase to refer to the Holy Ghost, then it is difficult to know how to read the Greek word translated "according to." What does it mean to say that Jesus has been determined or appointed to be the Son of God according to or by the Holy Ghost? As we saw in the discussion of *according to,* above, there are two possible answers. First, it could mean that the appointment to sonship was made through the power of the Holy Ghost. Second, it could

mean that Jesus' appointment is guaranteed by the Holy Ghost. I prefer the second answer, since it fits with the belief that any declaration of Christ's sonship comes through the Holy Ghost. The fact that this verse cites the resurrection as the means of that declaration is only a small problem, for it could still be true that the Holy Ghost declares Jesus to be the Son of God by means of the resurrection. In addition, if a reference to the Holy Ghost is intended, then the verse very nicely brings together each member of the Godhead in their work to save us. In spite of the odd phrasing, I think it reasonable to believe that Paul may be referring to the Holy Ghost here.

We have seen three possible ways of understanding the phrase *spirit of holiness*: It could tell us that Christ was appointed to be the Son of God because of his holy spirit. It could tell us that his appointment came by the power of the Holy Ghost. It could say that his appointment is guaranteed, or witnessed, by the Holy Ghost. The textual parallel of *spirit of holiness* with *flesh* suggests that the first of these three possibilities is the best. However, if one of the others is better, I think, as suggested above, that the last is most likely.

Given the ambiguities of the Greek text, there are at least two equally legitimate ways to translate this verse. Rather than insist on one or the other of them, consider each of them for its own merits:

> . . . who was declared to be the Son of God in a power that is in accordance with a spirit of holiness through the resurrection of the dead . . .

> . . . who was declared to be the Son of God in power, according to the Holy Spirit by means of the resurrection of the dead . . .

Other ambiguities might also alter the reading we could give this verse. As we have seen, for example, we can question what the

> And declared to be the Son of God with power, according to the spirit of holiness, by the resurrection from the dead:

phrase *in power* modifies. The KJV leaves this phrase ambiguous.

Ultimately, we cannot decide definitively how to read the phrase *spirit of holiness* or the other ambiguous phrases in this verse. Whatever other translations are possible, it remains true that the verse, like most scripture, is rich in material for thought and should not be reduced to an easy aphorism that we can master and memorize. The indeterminacy of this verse is not a defect, but a blessing. There is no reason to assume that one, and only one, appropriate reading of scripture exists. In fact, if we make that assumption, then the advice that we should continue to read and reread scripture is poor. If that assumption is true, then presumably, we could eventually discover the one correct reading. Having found that and understood it, there would be no further need of reading.

Jesus Christ our Lord

The phrase *Jesus Christ our Lord* is found in verse 3 of the King James translation and at the end of verse 4 of the alternate translation. This reflects a difference in the manuscripts used for translation. The King James translators used different manuscripts than those now generally believed to be authoritative. Though the King James translation places the phrase at the end of verse 3, the evidence, both textual and historical, supports the belief that this phrase belongs at the end of verse 4. Placed at the end of verse 4, the phrase stands in apposition to *his Son* (verse 3), with a long interjection between the two phrases. As we will see, *Jesus Christ our Lord* marks the end of a chiasm. To better understand why the phrase probably belongs at the end of verse 4,

consider this diagram of verses 3 and 4, given the alternate translation:

> ₃which [gospel] is about his|Son,
> who is from the seed of David according to the flesh,
> ₄but who was defined . . . according to the spirit . . .
> namely Jesus Christ our Lord

The end of verse 3, the beginning of verse 4, and the end of verse 4 are all appositive to the word *Son* in verse 3. If *Jesus Christ our Lord* is appositive to the beginning of verse 4, then the word order is significant. The apposition draws attention to the difference between *his Son* and *our Lord*. The Savior's relation to God is that of son; his relation to us is that of master. (For more about the word *Lord*, see Romans 10:9.)

The resurrection from the dead

The alternate translation gives a preferable reading of the phrase *the resurrection from the dead*: "the resurrection of the dead." Christ has been resurrected, as the King James translation indicates, but the point is that Christ's resurrection exemplifies and guarantees the resurrection of all others. By saying "resurrection of the dead," Paul indicates this. As Acts 4:2 and 23:6 show and as Latter-day revelation teaches, ancient Christians believed that Christ's resurrection was the first resurrection, the one that began the resurrection of all.

Verses 3–4

In the Greek text of verses 3 and 4 is an instance of a rhetorical convention called chiasmus.[59] Chiasmus is one of the many literary devices (rhetorical conventions) used by ancient writers to make speeches more pleasing and easier to understand and remember, as well as to emphasize elements of the speech. (This chiasm is evidence that verses 3 and 4 may have been part of an existing confession that Paul is quoting. Other Christians used such confessions and would have been familiar with the one that Paul is quoting here.) Ancient writers used many literary devices, but chiasmus is common and probably the one best known among Latter-day Saints. Chiasmus repeats ideas in inverted order, often using the same or similar words to mark the repetition. Chiasms are sometimes described as patterned ideas in the form a-b-b'-a', though longer chiasms are possible and common. We find a chiastic pattern in verses 3 and 4, outlined as follows:

A his Son
  B from the seed of David
    C according to the flesh
      X but who was declared/defined/
         appointed to be the Son of God in
         power
    C' according to the spirit
  B' from the resurrection of the dead
A' namely Jesus Christ our Lord

Note that I have translated the Greek text very literally to show the chiasm more clearly. Because the King James translation and my alternate translation are made to be readable in English, neither matches the chiastic pattern exactly. Note too that only the parts of this chiasm from A through B' are included in the King James Version, but the currently accepted edition of the manuscript allows us to add part A'. (See the discussion of *Jesus Christ our Lord* on page 26.)

This chiasm defines (or declares, see page 21) Christ by giving him a double genealogy, establishing the foundations of his sonship: it begins and ends by referring specifically to him. Its center point is the declaration or determination of him as Christ. Surrounding the center point are the elements that make up his being: flesh and spirit. The center point suggests what will overcome the gap illustrated by C and C', namely, the gap between

the flesh and the spirit, the gap between being a child of God and being, at best, the servant of the Son. This gap is overcome by the Son, in whom the spirit and the flesh come together. The Son was defined and appointed to be the one with the ability to bring us back to the Father, in the spirit and in the body, to be his children once again.

Though I find this proposed chiasm convincing, there are some who feel that chiasms do not occur at the phrase level. They feel that chiastic analysis is legitimate only insofar as it relates to clauses. Thus they would feel uncomfortable calling this a chiasm and would prefer to see it as a simple parallelism:

his Son, from the seed of David, according to
  the flesh,
but . . . the Son of God in power, according to
  the spirit.

We will see that those who believe this is a simple parallelism have prophetic evidence on their side.

JST Verse 4

And declared // the Son of God with power, by the Spirit according to the truth through the resurrection from the dead;

Before looking at verse 4 by itself, consider Joseph Smith's revision of verses 3 and 4. Joseph Smith's version makes the structure of these verses a parallelism instead of a chiasm:

A made of the seed of David
  B according to the flesh;
A declared the Son of God
  B by the Spirit

In this parallel, the phrases *with power* and *according to the truth through the resurrection from the dead* play subsidiary roles in the meaning of the two verses. The first modifies *declared* or *the Son of God* (but is ambiguous as to which). The second modifies *by the Spirit*.

> By whom we have received grace and apostleship, for obedience to the faith among all nations, for his name:

The Greek version of verses 3 and 4 centers on the declaration of Jesus as the Son of God. This declaration is the focal point of the proposed chiasm. In contrast, Joseph Smith's revision centers on the parallel between Christ's physical and spiritual genealogies. By deleting *to be*, the Prophet's version makes the word *declare* function more as the Greek word translated "declared" in the KJV functions— as a defining term rather than simply an annunciatory one. Joseph Smith removes the ambiguity of the phrase *spirit of holiness*, reading it as a reference to the Holy Ghost. He also clarifies that the Spirit is the means by which the declaration of Christ's sonship is made (see Romans 8:16), and by changing *by the resurrection* to *through the resurrection*, Joseph further clarifies that the Spirit makes this declaration by means of the resurrection.

Now consider verse 4 individually. In the Greek and King James versions of verse 4, the declaration of Jesus' sonship is made "according to the spirit of holiness." In the Prophet Joseph's version of the verse, declaration is made "according to the truth." In Joseph's rendering, *according to* seems to function like "in accordance with" rather than "in terms of" or "in relation to." The King James and Greek versions seem to favor the latter two meanings, though it is also possible to read the Joseph Smith version as saying that the declaration was made "in relation to the truth."

One way of reading the introduction of the notion of truth into verse 4 is as a further disambiguation of the ambiguous phrase *spirit of holiness*. Recall that the phrase can be read as both a name of the Holy Ghost and a description of Christ's spirit. As we have seen, Joseph Smith's translation indicates that the means by which Christ is declared the Son of God is the Holy Ghost rather than Christ's character. Perhaps "according to the truth" captures the other side of the ambiguity, the reference to Christ's character. After all, Christ refers to himself as "the truth" (see John 14:6; Ether 4:12), and many scriptures characterize him with truth (see, for example, John 1:14; Ephesians 4:21; Enos 1:26).

Though I find this solution to the question of by what means Jesus was declared the Son of God appealing, it is not conclusive. Both Christ and the Holy Ghost are called "the Spirit of truth" (see, for example, John 14:17; 15:26; and D&C 6:15 on the one hand and D&C 93:9 on the other hand). This indicates that the phrase *according to the truth* might be a continuation of the idea expressed by the phrase *by the Spirit* rather than a reference to Christ's character.

Verse 5

Like any other calling or blessing, apostleship brings duties and it requires faithfulness. The Lord was faithful in giving Paul the apostleship. Now Paul must in turn be faithful in receiving that gift.

We have received

In the phrase *we have received*, Paul could be using the plural *we* to include reference to his audience, but he is probably using the so-called writer's we that writers use to give their writing authority. Since Paul's authority is an issue in these opening verses, I believe that this is the most likely explanation of the plural pronoun.

Grace and apostleship

Paul has received grace and apostleship through Jesus Christ so that he can encourage faithful obedience among the gentiles for the sake of Christ's name. (Paul's calling is particularly to the gentiles. Of course, that does not mean he cannot preach to the Jews too. For other places where Paul connects grace with apostleship, see Romans 12:3; 15:15; 1 Corinthians 3:10; Galatians 2:9.) Paul begins and ends this letter by pointing out that the gospel leads people to faithful obedience: "Now to him that is of power to stablish you according to my gospel, and the preaching of Jesus Christ, according to the revelation of the mystery, which was kept secret since the world began, But now is made manifest, and by the scriptures of the prophets, according to the commandment of the everlasting God, *made known to all nations for the obedience of faith*" (Romans 16:25–26; italics added).

Not taking this connection seriously—either by thinking that faith does not require obedience or by assuming that obedience is enough for salvation—is the same as ignoring Paul's message.

The word translated "grace" (*charis*, χάρις) comes from a verb meaning "to show favor" or "to bestow a free gift." It has two senses: for the doer it means kindness or goodwill, and for the receiver it means thanks or gratitude.[60] Paul says he has received Christ's loving-kindness, in the form of a call to the apostleship (see Acts 9, 22; compare Romans 12:3; 15:15) so that he can work among the gentiles to bring about faith and the obedience that results from that faith.

Most Latter-day Saints understand what *apostleship* means (see the discussion of verse 1, pages 10–11), but the meaning of *grace* is less clear. Many both in the church and outside it use the word *grace* in contradistinction to *works*, as some interpretations of this letter assume. This verse shows the difficulty of making that distinction confidently. Paul has received grace ("kindness" or "goodness," see above) so that obedience—works—can come about in the world. Paul does not see

any opposition between grace and works, in other words, between faith—trusting the Lord so as to accept his gift—and obedience, when the grace and works come from Christ. Grace and works are both aspects of exactly the same thing, namely, the godly life.

Rather than speaking of grace and apostleship as two gifts given him by the Lord, Paul may be using a pleonastic pair, another rhetorical device that is sometimes also called hendiadys. A pleonastic pair is the use of two nouns connected by *and* to express one idea. Genesis 1:2, for example, says that the earth was "without form, and void." This is probably not a way of saying the earth was not only "without form, it was also empty." Rather, it is probably a way of saying, "without form; in other words, empty." Sometimes a pleonastic pair indicates a modifying relationship between two words. For example, Genesis 3:16 includes the phrase *thy sorrow and thy conception*. This is probably a pleonastic pair that could be translated, "the sorrow of thy conception." Similarly, *grace and apostleship* may be a pleonastic pair. Paul may be identifying God's grace with his call to the apostleship. We might also read the phrase as "the grace of apostleship," as it appears in the alternate translation. Given the miraculous nature of Paul's call, it would not be surprising for him to think of his calling in terms of grace (compare Acts 9:1–9).

The New Testament uses the Greek word *charisma* (χάρισμα), a variant of *charis* (χάρις), which is the word translated "grace," to describe the blessings and callings one receives by the laying on of hands, particularly the gift of the Holy Ghost (compare 1 Timothy 4:14; 2 Timothy 1:6). Grace is what we receive by being separated or set apart, as in the ordinance of confirmation or being set apart for a calling. Grace is a gift, a blessing (see the discussion of verse 1). This supports the view

> By whom we have received grace and apostleship, for obedience to the faith among all nations, for his name:

that *grace and apostleship* is a pleonastic pair. We could read this phrase to mean "the blessing of apostleship." According to this view, a calling is a spiritual gift. This may be surprising to those who tend to think of callings as spiritual obligations. Not only can those who receive callings be given gifts of the Spirit, but from Paul's point of view, a calling is itself a spiritual gift.

For obedience

As used here, the Greek word translated "for" means "in order to bring about." Paul has received grace and apostleship to bring about obedience among all humankind. Not only has the Lord decreed that Paul must obey and then help others obey, but God's loving-kindness to Paul has put Paul under a moral obligation to obey, and he must in turn give that loving-kindness to others, thereby putting them under the same moral obligation.

For example, if a person saves my life, then I am morally obliged to him, whether or not he asks for something in return. If I do something he asks of me, it is because I already owe him, not because I will receive something. He may in fact give me a gift in response to my service, but I have not earned it. I am actually more in his debt if he rewards me for what I have done for him. To use Paul's metaphor of slavery, the slave is obliged to obey not because of what he or she will get, but simply because that person is a slave. The slave is owned by the master and therefore owes whatever the master demands. If the master, being kind and loving, gives the slave a gift, that gift cannot be construed as something earned, for a slave can earn nothing from the master. Even if the master rewards

the slave in proportion to the work done or promises to reward the slave for his or her work, the slave has not *earned* that reward; the slave has acted as a slave acts, obediently, and the master has acted generously. Similarly, because we belong to the Father who created us and have been saved by Christ's loving-kindness, we are obliged to serve Christ and the Father. Paul's conversion experience shows us that contrary to popular wisdom, *love* and *obey* can be equivalents. Paul obeys because he loves. If we love fully, we will want to do the will of the Father; we will respond to Christ's loving-kindness with love. Conversely, when we do not want to do his will, we do not yet love fully.

The Savior connected love and obedience in John 14:15: "If ye love me, keep my commandments." The other side of this connection can be found in John 15:10: "If ye keep my commandments, ye shall abide in my love." We may be tempted to read the latter scripture to say that if we keep the commandments, then the Lord will love us, but the connection between obedience and love helps us see that this reading of the passage may be misleading. The Father loves us because we are his children, not because we serve him. If it were not so, few would be loved because few, if any, serve him sufficiently. John 15:10 speaks of Christ's love as if it were a home, a place of abode and protection. Christ tells us that we can remain in that place by keeping his commandments. He does not cease to love us when we disobey, but by disobeying we reject that love and refuse to abide in it. We cease to love him, and we leave him. In contrast, we continue to accept and thus to abide in his love when we obey.

In addition, "my love" is ambiguous in John 15:10. The most obvious way to read it is as referring to the Savior's love for us. It can also, however, be read as referring to our love for him, as if it said "love of me" instead of "my love." According to this reading, John 15:10 is a variation of John 14:15: we love Christ by obeying him.

Faith

Like *grace*, the word *faith* sometimes causes problems. We cannot define *faith* in short, simple terms because the word implies so much. Sometimes we hear it spoken of as if it were something absolutely foreign to our ordinary experience, perhaps akin to magic. But faith is not as mysterious as many would have it seem.

In the letter to the Romans, Paul uses various forms of the word *faith* that are often translated into English in other ways. For example, "belief" is a good translation for some of these cognate words (the King James translators use it often), and "trust" is another good translation. "Trust" is probably the most important meaning of the Greek word translated "faith" in verse 5 (*pistis*, πίστις). Unbelievers do not trust in God. Paul's message will bring them back to trusting him—if they will repent.

Even when it is appropriate to translate *pistis* as "faith" or "belief," the word also carries the connotation of trust.[61] To remind us of that connotation, the alternate translation uses the translation "trust" most often. If we keep the connections of "faith," "belief," and "trust" in mind as we read, we can see the connections Paul is making, connections that are not always obvious because the English words are not as clearly related to each other as the Greek words are. The alternate translation may help these relations stand out.

Obedience to the faith

There are a variety of ways to understand the phrase *obedience to the faith*. The King James translators show one understanding by translating the phrase this way rather than more literally. Literally, the Greek text says, "for obedience of faith." The question is, How are we to understand the word *of*? For example, we can speak of a religion as a faith, so one reading of this phrase is "obedience to the precepts taught in Christianity." But that seems not to be a New Testament use of the word *faith*, and the phrase can also mean "the obedience that is constituted by faith," "faithful obedience," or "obedience, in other words, faith." Given the content of the letter that follows this greeting, the first of these alternatives, "the obedience constituted by faith," seems most likely to me. If we have faith—in other words, trust—in the Lord, then we will do what that trust dictates. We will do what our Lord asks because we trust him. We will be obedient to our faith.

Among all nations

The Greek word translated "nations" literally means "nations"; the King James translation is literally correct. However, the Greek word is a translation of a Hebrew term having the specific meaning "gentiles." "Gentiles" has a good deal more content, for both Jews and Latter-day Saints, than does "nations." Hence, I have used "gentiles" in the alternate translation. Paul is speaking of his calling here. He has been called to preach the gospel among all the gentiles in order to bring about obedience to Christ among all people.

For his name

The Greek word translated "for" can mean "on behalf of," "concerned with," and "for the sake of" or "for his glory." Each of these seems applicable to Paul's work: he preaches on behalf of Christ, what he preaches is the good news that Christ has come to save us, and he preaches for the Savior's glory rather than his own.

Among whom are ye also the called of Jesus Christ: To all that be in Rome, beloved of God, called to be saints: Grace to you and peace from God our Father, and the Lord Jesus Christ.

JST Verse 5

By whom we have received grace and apostleship, <u>through</u> obedience, <u>and</u> faith <u>in his name, to preach the gospel</u> among all nations //;

Joseph Smith changes the preposition *for* to *through*. The Greek preposition indicates that obedience is the object or goal of Paul's receipt of grace and apostleship. Joseph Smith's translation makes obedience the means by which Paul obtained grace and apostleship, though that is strange, considering his former persecution of the Christians. The other changes in the verse, however, make it clear that Paul's call was a consequence of obedience and faith. The Prophet has changed the verse so that it unmistakably says that Paul received his call as an apostle to the gentiles *through* his obedience and faith in Christ. Strange as it may seem at first glance, the Prophet Joseph Smith's revision of this verse seems to indicate that Paul was obedient and had faith in Jesus' name before his conversion.

It is possible to see this as an early version of a theme that Paul takes up in detail in verse 19 and continues to discuss into chapter 2, namely, how those who do not keep the law can be saved. If those who disobey the law can have a knowledge of God, then it is reasonable to say that non-Christians live by obedience—and even by faith in the name of Christ, since they have the light of Christ—when they live by their best lights. In spite of his persecution of the Christians, Paul was clearly faithful prior to his conversion in that he did what he sincerely believed was in ac-

cordance with the law of God. In fact, Paul's conversion is a good indication that his persecution of the Christians was motivated by his obedience to the law and his faith in God rather than by personal gain. Immediately after seeing that he was mistaken, Paul changed his allegiance. It might be better to say that Paul changed the outward form of his allegiance but remained as faithful as he had ever been. That he was immediately willing to obey and be faithful to Christ after receiving a revelation that he had been persecuting God the Son is strong evidence that by being faithful to what God had manifested to him (see verse 19), Paul was already, though unknowingly, obedient and faithful to Christ.

If such an understanding of Joseph Smith's translation of this verse is correct, it sheds a different light on our judgments of one another. We can assume very little about the faithfulness of others, even of those who are our persecutors. The admonition not to condemn others (see Matthew 7:1; Luke 6:37; 3 Nephi 14:1; John 7:24) and the command to pray for those who persecute us (see Matthew 5:44; Luke 6:28; 3 Nephi 12:44) take on new meaning when we see that even our persecutors may be obedient and faithful in their persecution. Those we think of as our enemies may, like Paul, be exercising exemplary obedience and faithfulness, misguided though it may be.

Verse 6

Verse 6 is the last verse of the parenthetical comment that began in verse 2.

Among

The word *among* is equivocal. It could mean either "living amidst" or "one of." As we will see shortly, Paul's sermon provokes the complacent Roman saints. Paul begins this provocation by being unclear about whether he means that the Roman saints are among the gentiles merely because that is where they live or because they are in a spiritual sense "among the nations" rather than in the community of the children of God.

The called of Jesus Christ

The idea of the phrase *the called of Jesus Christ* is parallel to that of a similar phrase in verse 1 (see *called to be an apostle*, page 10) and also appears in verse 7 (see *called to be saints*, pages 36–37). The saints in Rome are called of Jesus Christ; their membership in the Lord's church is a calling.

There are several ways to read the phrase *the called of Jesus Christ*. It could mean "those called by the name of Christ," "those called by Christ," or "those called who belong to Jesus Christ." In this phrase, as we have already seen in other places, the ambiguity is fruitful. It opens up the verse to our thought rather than closing it off.

JST Verse 6

Among whom <u>are ye also</u> // called of Jesus Christ;

Joseph Smith changes only the word order and drops the word *the*. He seems to be making the King James English fit the usage of nineteenth-century America more closely and thus making it more readily comprehensible to the saints.

Verses 1–6

In verses 1–6 there is an interesting progression of ideas. Paul mentions in verse 1 that he is an apostle. In verse 2 he explains obliquely that being an apostle or prophet means preaching the gospel. In verses 3 and 4 he tells us what that gospel is. Finally, in verses 5 and 6, he comes back to his calling as an apostle and says that it is particularly a calling to the gentiles, including the Roman

saints. Paul begins with himself and moves toward increasingly wider spheres—to apostleship, to the gospel, and to the Lord and his work, including the rest of the members of the church.

Notice how the themes of separation, spirit and spirituality, and holiness run through these verses. We can see at least five related claims:

1. What is separated within or to the gospel is spiritual.
2. What is spiritual is holy.
3. Christ has been set apart, defined, or declared to be the Son of God "in accordance with" the spirit of holiness.
4. Paul has been separated or defined (presumably by his calling) to the gospel as a servant to preach the good news of Christ.
5. The saints are called in the gospel to be holy.

Verse 7

To all that be in Rome

After the long digression in verses 2–6, we finally come to Paul's address of those to whom he is writing. Presumably he is writing to the Roman saints, but the phrase *to all that be in Rome* leaves open the possibility that his address is, at least in principle, meant for everyone in Rome. In addition, as a synecdoche (using a part of something to stand for the whole), Rome may stand for the world as a whole.

Beloved of God

The phrase *beloved of God* means "Christians." The word translated "beloved" (*agapētos*, ἀγαπητός) is used in three ways in the New Testament: as a description of Christ (see Matthew 3:17), as a description of fellow saints (see 1 Corinthians 4:14), and as a term of address or salutation (see 1 John 2:7, where the King James translation has "brethren"). In

> To all that be in Rome, beloved of God, called to be saints: Grace to you and peace from God our Father, and the Lord Jesus Christ.

Greek sources outside the Judeo-Christian religious tradition, the root of the word translated "beloved," namely, *agapē* (ἀγάπη), is not particularly interesting.[62] It denotes satisfaction and preference and a love that makes distinctions. Possibly because the Septuagint favors the word *beloved* in its translation of the Old Testament, Christianity emphasizes the word and its relatives. (See the discussions of verse 1, page 4, and verse 17, pages 65–66, for more on the Septuagint.) The Greek word *agapē* denotes what in the Old Testament is usually denoted by the Hebrew word *ʾaheb* (אָהֵב). In the Septuagint the word *agapē* is used for marital love (as in Genesis 29:32), for the love of God (as in Exodus 20:6), and for one's obligation to one's neighbor (for example, Leviticus 19:18). Though the meaning of *agapē* varies, the love denoted is usually particular rather than universal and is concrete rather than abstract.

Sometimes people say that the New Testament distinguishes between *agapē* (ἀγάπη) and *erōs* (ἔρως) and that the former is Christian love while the latter is erotic love. The point seems to have reached almost canonized status in Latter-day Saint Sunday School teaching. Nevertheless, I believe that distinction was made by well-meaning clerics and adopted by us but is not a distinction in New Testament Greek. After all, the translators of the Septuagint use the word *agapē* for the Hebrew word *ʾaheb* in each of its senses, including marital or sexual love (see for example, Song of Solomon 7:6 [verse 7 in the Septuagint]; 8:6–7.) It would be surprising if the variety of meanings in the Old Testament did not carry over into New Testament use. Little evidence exists for the distinction in the New Testament.

However, the New Testament gives a new reading of the Old Testament notion of love, particularly in its emphasis on God's love as pardoning and in its insistence that love of the neighbor is not preferential. As the parable of the good Samaritan shows, the love recommended in the New Testament is particular and concrete rather than universal and abstract. It is not enough to love everyone in a general sense. We must love those with whom we associate personally, our neighbor. As the parable of the good Samaritan also shows, Christian love is not restrictive as to who the neighbor is. Proximity seems enough to make someone our neighbor.

The phrase *beloved of God* continues the connotation of preference. Though in one sense God loves every person, in another sense *beloved of God* applies exclusively to the saints, not by virtue of their purity, but by virtue of their calling as saints (see, for example, Deuteronomy 7:13, where the Lord speaks of Israel as those whom he loves). On the other hand, the ambiguity of *among all nations* (verse 5) may be repeated here: though the obvious referent is the church in Rome, those not yet in the church may also be implied.

It is interesting that Paul identifies the saints not by their love for God or by their love for each other, but by the divine love for them. We must love both God and our neighbor (Matthew 22:37–39), but as we will see, our love for God and our neighbor is made possible by God's love for us. Our love for him does not make us saints; rather, his love calls us to be saints.

Saints

The Greek word translated "saint" (*hagios*, ἅγιος) means "one devoted to the gods" and indicates purity of character. It is a cognate of the Greek word for *holy*. In the Old Testament, the Hebrew word for *holy* (*qodesh*, קֹדֶשׁ, the same word used in the phrase *spirit of holiness* [see pages 24–25]) is used mostly to refer to God, but it can also be used in other ways. The Old Testament refers not just to God, but to both people and things as being holy (see, for example, Exodus 3:5; 19:14 [translated "sanctified"]; 26:33; Leviticus 19:2; Isaiah 48:2; 62:12; 64:10). When used to refer to people or things, the word *holy* means something like "set apart for holy purposes," often purposes of temple ritual.[63] Because holy objects have been set apart, they can be used properly only in certain ways. Holiness derives from being set apart, not from the character of the object in question. For example, the altar is holy because it has been set apart for use in the temple, not because it has a certain shape or is made of a particular material. Any use of the altar not in line with its prescribed use as a holy object is forbidden.[64] Similarly, Israel is holy because it is chosen, not the reverse. Being called and set apart for particular divine purposes makes Israel holy, and that holiness puts her under the solemn and divine obligation to live up to the holiness to which she has been set apart. If Israel obeys God, that obedience is the proper response to her calling—to the fact that she is holy—but it is not what makes her holy. This interpretation of the Old Testament concept of holiness is crucial to understanding what Paul has to say in his letter to the Romans, because he develops that notion and shows how it applies within the new context created by the coming of Christ and his atonement. The subtitle of Paul's letter could easily be "On Sanctification" or "On What It Means to Be Holy."

We can see this interest in and emphasis on sanctification throughout the greeting that ends in verse 7. Verse 2 notes that the holy scriptures testify of the gospel. Verse 4 speaks of the holy spirit, meaning either Christ's character or the being who testifies of Christ.

Now verse 7 says that Paul's audience is called to be holy.

Surely the purity of character identified with saintliness is at least part of what Paul intends. Those in Rome have been called to be pure. That is expected of them. But given the connotations of the word *saint* in the Old Testament, we must remember that *saint* describes not just moral cleanliness (in the broadest sense), but also and especially a particular covenant relation to God. The chosen people—saints in the New Testament and today—are those who enter into covenant. In Exodus 19:3–6, the Lord covenants with Israel. Those verses teach that *by entering into the covenant* (rather than because of their purity) Israel will become a holy nation. *Holy nation* in Exodus 19:6 could also be translated "nation of saints" (*goy qadosh*, גּוֹי קָדוֹשׁ). Just as holy objects are those set aside for holy purposes, the saints are set aside for God's holy purposes. Therefore, a reasonable translation of the Greek word *hagios* might be "one of God's people." It may be that Paul is using *saint* as a parallel to *bondman* or *slave*, which appear in the first verse: a saint is a bondman of God, one who belongs to him and who owes him work. As such, the saint is holy and, therefore, is obligated to God to be pure.

Though in scripture holiness has more to do with being called than with actions, the calling to be a saint carries with it the obligation to be pure. As we have seen from verse 6 and as King Benjamin teaches (see Mosiah 5), to be a saint means to be worthily called by the name of Christ. That the Greek word for *saint* indicates purity shows that there is more to being a saint, to taking Christ's name upon ourselves, than membership in the formal organization of the church. We become saints by being called and set apart for God's purposes, and we remain saints by striving to meet the obligation of purity that such a calling

> To all that be in Rome, beloved of God, called to be saints: Grace to you and peace from God our Father, and the Lord Jesus Christ.

entails. Severance from among the saints, formal excommunication, is therefore not a matter of saying that the excommunicated person is no longer pure. That implies the obviously false claim that those in the church are pure. Rather, excommunication is a pronouncement that the excommunicate has in some way given up his or her calling as a saint. To excommunicate a person is to judge that the person has gone beyond the limits that define membership in the church. It is to judge that the person has ceased to work to fulfill God's purposes by refusing the obligation of obedience that comes with the call to saintliness. Only by being purified can anyone be worthy of Christ's name, and we cannot purify ourselves. However, accepting the call to fulfill divine purposes qualifies a person for a token of purity, the token we share by being formal members of Christ's church, by being called saints. As part of our calling as saints, we are set apart to holy callings.

Interestingly, the word *saint* does not appear in the New Testament in the singular. In fact, in all the standard works, *saint* occurs in the singular only once, in Mosiah 3:19. As Benjamin makes clear, Christ's redemption and our humble submission to him make us saints. Perhaps the word is used almost exclusively in the plural to remind us that our membership in the community of saints is a token of the possibility that we can become true saints, though we are not yet saints as individuals. Or perhaps it is plural so that we will not forget that we cannot become saints alone. We can become pure only through Jesus Christ and with the help of other saints, particularly our ancestors (see D&C 128:15). An individual would be presumptuous to claim

to be a saint, because such a declaration implies a claim to purity that is not in keeping with acknowledging our nothingness before the Lord (see Mosiah 4:11). Saintliness requires humility and a recognition that we are utterly dependent on God. It is even more presumptuous to declare any individual besides Christ to be a saint if by *saint* we mean "one who is pure." However, if by calling ourselves saints we indicate our membership in the church, our communion with the rest of those who intend to live as God's people, and our calling to the service of God, it is not presumptuous to claim to be saints.

Called to be saints

The phrase *called to be saints* is literally translated "called saints." It is grammatically parallel to a phrase like *green bench*. As we have just seen, the saints in Rome are saints by virtue of their calling, not by virtue of their purity. Grammatically, the Greek phrase is exactly parallel to "called apostle" in verse 1: Paul compares his calling as an apostle to the Romans' calling as saints. The parallel suggests something like "You are called to be saints, just as I am called to be an apostle." Compare Romans 8:28–29; 9:24; 1 Corinthians 1:9; and especially 2 Timothy 1:9–10: "Who hath saved us, and called us with an holy calling, not according to our works, but according to his own purpose and grace, which was given us in Christ Jesus before the world began, but is now made manifest by the appearing of our Saviour Jesus Christ, who hath abolished death, and hath brought life and immortality to light through the gospel." To what have both Paul and the Roman saints been called? Certainly not to Christianity. The callings to be an apostle and to be a saint come to those who are already Christians. The answer seems to be that each is ultimately called to sainthood, to holiness, to purity, to sanctification. Along with *slave*, the word *saints* (and its cognates, seen in words translated "holy" and "holiness") is one of the key words of Paul's introduction. *Slave* and *saints* set the themes that Paul will explicate in the letter: how by being God's slaves we may become his saints, his holy children.

The gospel is the good news that we can overcome the bad news of the fall, which alienated us from God because of sin. It is the good news that we are already holy in an important sense, namely, as God's instruments. We are called and set apart by our baptism and confirmation to be servants of God. The gospel is the promise that we can be purified and eventually become once again the sons and daughters of God. As verse 6 points out, when we hear that news, we receive a call to participate in a life that is reconciled to our Heavenly Father and to become one of his people, one of the saints. When we hear the gospel message, the only appropriate life is a saintly life. Any other life (any life that includes sin) insists on continuing the alienation from God and from our spiritual selves (see the discussion of *flesh* in verse 3, pages 19–20). Since alienation from God is overcome through the gospel and since the gospel is freely given to us, if we insist on anything other than a life of obedience, we deny the atonement.

Much of Paul's discussion in this letter seems to be an attempt to explain to those called to be saints what that calling entails. As mentioned earlier, the etymological connection between the Greek words translated "holy" and "saint" suggests that the calling to be a saint may be a reference to Leviticus 19:2: "Ye shall be holy: for I the Lord your God am holy." (See the discussion of verse 4, page 22.) Paul wants us to be saints in fact as well as in name, and in this letter he strives, in the words of verse 5, to show us what the obedi-

ence of faith is. He does this by showing what the relation between faith and works is and how many dissemble faithful obedience, as if they could wrest salvation from God by their works. When he speaks negatively of works, as is clear in the other chapters of Romans, he is speaking of the dissimulation of faithful obedience.

Peace

If we pay attention to the word *peace* in a later reading of the letter, it changes character. In the first reading, it is possible to read Paul's prayer for peace quite straightforwardly: Paul wishes them peace. But once we have read the whole letter and see that much of it criticizes the present character of the saints, the word *peace* becomes ironic. It is as if Paul is saying, "I bring you peace, but when all is said and done, many of you may not recognize what I bring as peace. It may seem much more like war." The peace that Paul offers the Roman saints is what will come through his call to repentance, something that may not make them very comfortable. He preaches a peace that disrupts the complacent and comfortable "peace" into which they may have fallen.

Grace to you and peace

Fitzmyer suggests that the phrase *grace to you and peace* may be an echo of the Levitical blessing found in Numbers 6:24–26: "The Lord bless thee, and keep thee: the Lord make his face shine upon thee, and be gracious unto thee: the Lord lift up his countenance upon thee, and give thee peace," a blessing still used formally in many Christian churches.[65] However, it may not be a direct echo of that passage. Perhaps the standard Hebrew greeting (see page 2) is an echo of the blessing in Numbers and Paul is varying the standard greeting.

In any case, Paul's usage is not standard,

> To all that be in Rome, beloved of God, called to be saints: Grace to you and peace from God our Father, and the Lord Jesus Christ.

suggesting that this may be a pleonastic pair: perhaps *grace* and *peace* are to be understood as synonyms, or perhaps we should read this as "the grace of peace to you" (see the discussion of the pleonastic pair *grace and apostleship* in verse 5, page 29). Presumably, the grace that Paul offers consists of his kindness or goodness and the kindness and goodness of Christ that he brings as the Lord's messenger. As we have seen, the peace he offers is the peace of the gospel.

Compare this mention of grace and peace to verse 5: Paul has received grace and apostleship, and he now offers grace and peace. The parallel this creates between *apostleship* and *peace* may suggest several things. For example, it may remind us that Paul received spiritual peace through his call to be an apostle, a messenger of Christ. That peace is something he can now give to others by being faithful to his calling as an apostle, and it is something that they can receive by being faithful to their calling as saints. The parallel may show that just as the gift of apostleship that Paul received necessitated his service, so the grace that the Roman saints have received—the gift of the gospel—and what they will receive from Paul in this letter necessitates their service. Similarly, perhaps the parallel can remind us that just as Paul was made into something new by the grace he received, so are we made into something new—sons and daughters of Christ—when we genuinely receive the grace that Christ offers. If we remember the meaning of the word *apostle*, namely, "messenger," the parallel between *peace* and *apostleship* may remind us that peace comes through preaching and living the gospel.

Whatever we make of this parallel, to be a Christian is to receive grace and peace. Paul's letter is a discourse on grace and peace: the grace—gift or favor—available from God through his son, Jesus Christ, and the peace that comes through accepting that grace.

In addition, as mentioned in the discussion of verse 1 (see page 2), Jewish letters usually began with an offer of peace: "from ——— to ———, peace." By adding *grace* to the usual salutation, Paul emphasizes his relationship to Christ, which distinguishes him from the Jews who do not believe. Given the connection of grace and apostleship in verse 5, by adding *grace* to the usual greeting, Paul offers them his work as an apostle. He offers to bear witness of Christ by preaching the gospel. By referring to his call, Paul offers to others what he has received.

From God our Father, and the Lord Jesus Christ

As evident in the phrase *from God our Father, and the Lord Jesus Christ,* Paul refers to the Father and the Son as distinct entities. The blessings of the gospel come from both.

JST Verse 7

To all that be in Rome, beloved of God, called // saints: Grace to you and peace from God our Father, and the Lord Jesus Christ.

The Prophet Joseph's version of this verse deletes *to be,* making more obvious what we have noticed in the Greek text, that *called* is an adjective describing *saints.*

Verses 8–15

King James

8First, I thank my God through Jesus Christ for you all, that your faith is spoken of throughout the whole world. 9For God is my witness, whom I serve with my spirit in the gospel of his Son, that without ceasing I make mention of you always in my prayers; 10Making request, if by any means now at length I might have a prosperous journey by the will of God to come unto you. 11For I long to see you, that I may impart unto you some spiritual gift, to the end ye may be established; 12That is, that I may be comforted together with you by the mutual faith both of you and me. 13Now I would not have you ignorant, brethren, that oftentimes I purposed to come unto you, (but was let hitherto,) that I might have some fruit among you also, even as among other Gentiles. 14I am debtor both to the Greeks and the Barbarians; both to the wise, and to the unwise. 15So, as much as in me is, I am ready to preach the gospel to you that are at Rome also.

Alternate

8Chiefly, I thank my God through Jesus Christ for all of you, because your faith is spoken of in the whole world. 9God, whom I serve spiritually in preaching the gospel of his Son, is my witness of how I mention you unceasingly; 10always in my prayers I ask whether now, at last, I will be blessed by God's will to come to you. 11For I long to see you so that I can share some spiritual gift with you so that you may be strengthened. 12This gift is that I will be strengthened with you through the trust we share, your trust and mine. 13However, I do not wish you to be ignorant, brothers: I often intended to come to you so that I might have some fruit among you, too, even as I have had among the other gentiles, but I was prevented until the present. 14I am a debtor to Greeks and non-Greeks, to the wise and the foolish; 15thus, for my part, I am eager to preach the gospel also to you in Rome.

First, I thank my God through Jesus Christ for you all, that your faith is spoken of throughout the whole world.

Verse 8

To this point Paul's address has been somewhat formal. In verse 8 it becomes more personal. Paul wants the Romans to know and understand him not only because of his official position, but also because of his interest in them.

In verse 7, Paul sent grace to the saints in Rome, and verse 8 shows part of what that grace includes. Remember that grace includes not only kindness or a gift, but thankfulness as well (see the discussion of verse 5, page 29). Thankfulness is part of the grace Paul sends them.

First

First can mean "the first thing I want to say is . . ." Yet this word can be taken not just as a marker for the first item in a list, but, as shown in the alternate translation, it can also mean "chiefly." Since no other elements of a list appear in the letter, "chiefly" seems to capture the meaning more clearly.

I thank

The root of the word translated "I thank" (*eucharisteō*, εὐχαριστέω) is *charis* (χάρις), meaning "grace." The grace of thanks is Paul's response to the grace of God.

As a side note, many Christians refer to what Latter-day Saints call the sacrament (presumably short for the sacrament of the Lord's supper) as the Eucharist. In so doing, they recognize that the sacrament is a sacrament of grace. Our sacrament prayers make this explicit in asking that the bread and water be blessed and sanctified to the souls of those who partake of them.

Paul begins most of his letters with thanks and, somewhat less often, blessings (see 1 Corinthians 1:4; Philippians 1:3; Colossians 1:3; 1 Thessalonians 1:2; 2 Thessalonians 1:3; Philemon 1:4 for similar thanks; and see 2 Corinthians 1:3–4; Ephesians 1:3 for blessings). Notice, however, that Galatians offers neither thanks nor blessings, a fact that is undoubtedly associated with the context in which that letter was written.

I thank my God through Jesus Christ

The blessing to the saints comes through two beings, the Father and the Son, and Paul prays to the Father through Jesus Christ.

That your faith

The word *that* has the sense of "because" in the phrase *that your faith*. That the Roman saints are well-known is a cause for gratitude.

Your faith is spoken of throughout the whole world

Rome was considered in the West to be the center of the world, and the Roman saints were part of "a city that is set on a hill" (Matthew 5:14). It is not clear whether Paul is grateful that all people know that there is a Christian congregation in Rome, whether he is grateful that the saints in other locations know about the Roman congregation, or whether he is grateful that the saints in Rome have made a good name for Christianity. Because in Romans 2 Paul makes what can be taken as a strong criticism of the Roman saints, we might be tempted to assume that he means only the first: he is grateful that people know that there is a congregation in Rome. However, the criticism Paul levies in chapter 2 is the kind that can be brought against almost all Christians at any time and at any place, and it is directed at "someone" or "anyone who would say such and such" rather than at a particular person or group. It seems unreasonable to suppose that Paul thinks the Roman Christians have made a poor name for the church. If we include the idea that both all people and other saints are aware of the Roman congregation in our understanding of verse 8, then from the phrase *your faith is spoken of throughout the whole world* we can conclude that Paul believes that it is good that Christians are in Rome and that both Christians and non-Christians know that they are. Surely that would help in missionary work. In addition, Paul is grateful that the saints have made a good reputation for Christians.

There is another way of understanding the phrase *your faith is spoken of throughout the whole world*. Perhaps Paul is using hyperbole, or exaggeration, to carry on the theme he began in verse 6: these men and women are known for their faith. Not only have they taken on themselves the name of Christ and thereby become known among believers as people of faith, but they are also known for their faith among those who do not believe.

Perhaps this letter is addressed to those in obvious need of repentance, maybe even those guilty of the sins described at the end of Romans 1. If this reading is correct, Paul's compliment is backhanded. Because he has never been to Rome, he can know the saints there only by reputation, and a worldly reputation is something of which we must beware (see 1 Nephi 13:8–9). Perhaps by knowing that they are renowned for their faith, Paul knows he must call them to repentance. However, this suggestion seems unlikely. After all, Paul begins his letter by dwelling on the fact that these people are well-known for their faith, not only to him (see verse 6), but to the world in general. This letter is to those who are already obedient, at least in the eyes of most, but who nonetheless stand in need of repentance.

What Paul says is not what he would say to those who are not yet Christians; he speaks to those who are already thought of as faithful members. This message to those known for their faith and obedience is important not only to the saints in Paul's time, but to Latter-day Saints as well. However, the message has relatively little to say to those who have not yet taken Christ's name on themselves, who are not yet "called saints" (see the discussion of verse 7, pages 36–37). This letter is less like a missionary tract and more like an address in stake or general conference, an address to those who have already taken Christ's name on themselves through covenant.

JST Verse 8

First, I thank my God through Jesus Christ, <u>that you are all steadfast</u>, and your faith is spoken of throughout the whole world.

By changing *for you all* to *that you are all steadfast*, the Joseph Smith revision creates a parallel: *you are all steadfast* is parallel to the Roman's exemplary faith "spoken of throughout the whole world." This draws our attention to the faithfulness of the saints in Rome, creating an even stronger contrast between their faithfulness and Paul's calling them to repentance than does the Greek text or the King James translation.

This contrast makes it more apparent that the book of Romans is for the saints of any time. Rather than speaking to those still outside the church, Paul speaks, according to the Joseph Smith Translation, to those who have already been baptized, those who have already accepted the gospel and its obligations. It is they who stand in need of conversion, not to Christianity, but within Christianity to genuine faith in Christ. They are already Christians in name, but now they need to be sanctified; in other words, they need to become

> For God is my witness, whom I serve with my spirit in the gospel of his Son, that without ceasing I make mention of you always in my prayers;

fully Christian. The work of Paul is much the same as that of Alma (see Alma 5:14–42), namely, calling those within the church to recognize the full meaning of their membership.

Verse 9

For

The Greek word translated "for" (gar, γάρ) is a weak connective that is often used as we might use *and* in conversation: to continue without necessarily indicating a particular logical connection between what came before and what comes next.[66] The alternate translation leaves the word untranslated because it does not contribute significantly to the sense of the passage and could even be misleading.

God is my witness

The Greek word for *witness* (martus, μάρτυς) is also the root of the English word *martyr*. To us *martyr* means something like "one who dies for a cause" or perhaps "one who bears testimony of the truth by dying for it," but the Greek word signifies merely "one who can or should testify to something." Thus the word *martus* can also be translated as a word we hear more commonly: *testimony*. A testimony is something we say to establish the truth. Since the Roman saints do not know Paul personally and therefore cannot directly know of his love for them, God bears testimony to them through the Holy Ghost that Paul prays for the saints continually.

Serve

The Greek word *latreuō* (λατρεύω) means "service to the gods" or "worship." The

Septuagint always uses the word to refer to religious service, whether to God or idols. It is used in Exodus 12:26 (to mean "service") and 1 Chronicles 28:13 (where it refers to the "vessels of service" in the tabernacle). Although this Greek word for *service* does not share a root with the Greek word for *saint*, both imply the same idea, namely, service to the gods. As 1 Chronicles 28:13 shows, temple service is one of the connotations of the word *serve*, though I doubt it is relevant to this verse since the context is unrelated to temple service.

A different connection to temple service is nonetheless evident. By using a word that connotes temple service, Paul points out that his service is a form of worship: he honors God by the service he renders as an apostle. In that sense, any service to the Divine is worship, whether partaking of the sacrament in a worship meeting, working in the stake cannery or on the welfare farm, teaching in the Primary, or visiting and home teaching. Paul teaches the same concept as King Benjamin: "When ye are in the service of your fellow beings ye are only in the service of your God" (Mosiah 2:18).

Spirit

The meaning of the Greek word translated "spirit" (pneuma, πνεῦμα) is similar to the traditional notion of soul or the Latter-day Saint understanding of the spirit. The Greek word, however, can be more broadly translated "mind," though the KJV does not use this particular translation. *Pneuma* refers to the knowing and willing self and is also the word translated "ghost" in KJV references to the Holy Ghost. (For more on *pneuma*, see the commentary on verse 11, page 46.)

I serve with my spirit

The alternate translation renders the phrase *I serve with my spirit* as "I serve spiritually." A major theme of this letter is the contrast between the spirit and the flesh. Earlier Paul spoke of Christ's ancestry according to the flesh (see verse 3) and the spirit (see verse 4). In so doing he showed that he is talking not about dichotomy between the flesh and the spirit or between works and faith, but about a unity between them. In verse 9 Paul talks similarly about his own service in the spirit. If the letter contained this absolute dichotomy that some read into it and deduce from scriptures such as Galatians 6:7–8, then Paul would be loath to associate Christ with the flesh and himself with the spirit. That he makes both these associations shows, again, that he does not see the flesh and the spirit as necessarily opposed to one another—except in the unrepentant. Because the unrepentant find the flesh and the spirit, the living body, to be necessarily opposed, conflicted, and self-alienated, they do not find the reconciliation of works and grace that the repentant find. To those who are repentant, grace and works—or the spirit and the body—are ultimately each two ways of talking about the same thing, even if, in a fallen world, they sometimes seem irreconcilable. (However, as we see in Romans 7 and the beginning of Romans 8, Paul sometimes uses the word *flesh* to indicate what we today might call the unrepentant or fallen soul.)

Paul's spiritual service also anticipates the spiritual gift mentioned in verse 11; he serves in the spirit so that he can deliver a spiritual gift to the Romans. Paul also draws a parallel between himself and Christ: because the Son is defined by the spirit of holiness, Paul, as the slave of Jesus Christ, must serve in that spirit, and he serves to call us to that spirit.

When Paul says that he serves or worships God in his spirit, he is not saying that he worships only inwardly, ignoring ordinances and works. Were that the case, he

would not have taken the Nazarite vows (see the discussion on page 12). Neither would the admonitions of Romans 12–15 make any sense. Instead, Paul worships with his whole being by preaching the gospel.

JST Verse 9

For God is my witness, whom I serve / /, that without ceasing I make mention of you always in my prayers, <u>that you may be kept through the Spirit, in the gospel of his Son,</u>

The deletion of *in my spirit* lessens the impact of Paul's service on the verse and erases the ironic parallel of Christ's flesh and Paul's spirit (see the discussion of *I serve in my spirit*, above). Joseph Smith's revision also moves the rest of the deletion, *in the gospel of his Son*, to the end of the verse and makes it part of the object of Paul's prayers: "that you may be kept through the Spirit, in the gospel of his Son." This changes the character of the verse considerably. The King James and Greek texts make a point of Paul's praying continually for the saints in Rome, while the Joseph Smith Translation focuses on Paul's prayers that the saints be kept through the Spirit.

Normal word order for the phrase *that you may be kept through the Spirit, in the gospel of his Son* would be "that you may be kept in the gospel of his Son through the Spirit." What are we to make of the inverted word order in Joseph Smith's translation? Rather than emphasizing that Paul desires the Roman saints to be kept in the gospel, the inverted word order emphasizes that they are to be kept by means of the Spirit. The *Oxford English Dictionary* and the 1828 edition of Webster's *American Dictionary of the English Language* tell us that in this context in the nineteenth century, *kept* could mean "to guard, defend, protect," "to maintain or preserve in proper order," "to provide for the sustenance of," "to tend; to

> Making request, if by any means now at length I might have a prosperous journey by the will of God to come unto you.

have the care of," "to preserve in being or operation," or "to retain in one's power or control."[67] We can therefore understand the addition to mean that Paul prays that

1. the saints of Rome will be protected and sustained in the gospel;
2. they will be maintained in the order given them by the gospel—perhaps the order of the church, perhaps the order of a gospel life;
3. the saints will be preserved as followers of the gospel;
4. and within the gospel, the saints will remain under the influence of the Holy Spirit.

Joseph Smith's revision suggests a possible change of emphasis in the letter as a whole. It suggests that the letter is perhaps intended not as an explanation of sanctification, but as a means of strengthening the members of the church in Rome. If we take the letter as a discourse on sanctification, then we read it to say something like "Although you are known throughout the world for your faith, you do not yet understand sanctification." According to the reading suggested by the Prophet's revision of this verse, in spite of the renown of the saints, their faith needs to be strengthened (verse 11 may support this understanding of the purpose of the letter). Of course, the letter may also be some combination of both purposes: an explanation of sanctification and a letter intended to strengthen the saints' faith.

Verse 10

To come unto you

In his prayers Paul has asked whether he might be permitted to "come unto" Rome to preach the gospel. It appears he has been asking for some time and has so far been refused. The King James translation seems to indicate that Paul has been requesting permission to make an actual visit to Rome, but in the Greek that is not clearly the case. It is ambiguous whether Paul's prayer has been for a visit or simply for contact with the Roman saints. In the latter case, the idea of a journey is a metaphor and this letter is Paul's way of coming to them. It is what he would say to them if he came in person. As we will see in Romans 15:24, however, Paul would like to visit the Romans on his way to Spain—if he can. Though the King James Version takes a definite stand on the question of whether Paul is speaking of an actual visit to Rome, at this point in the letter the Greek is ambiguous.

Have a prosperous journey

Strictly and etymologically interpreted, the Greek word *euodoō* (εὐοδόω) means "to have a prosperous journey." This meaning is the basis for the King James translation. However, in the Greek of Paul's time, the phrase *have a prosperous journey* could also mean "to have success in general," as it probably does here.[68] (For similar uses, see 1 Corinthians 16:2–3; 3 John 1:2.) The alternate translation uses "blessed."

By the will of God

Because, by virtue of their membership in the church, all saints have always already come together in spirit, even if not physically, Paul needs to come to Rome himself only if the Father wills it. Members of the church have a fellowship that is described in the greeting of the school of the prophets: "Art thou a brother or brethren? I salute you in the name of the Lord Jesus Christ, in token or remembrance of the everlasting covenant, in which covenant I receive you to fellowship, in a determination that is fixed, immovable, and unchangeable, to be your friend and brother through the grace of God in the bonds of love, to walk in all the commandments of God blameless, in thanksgiving, forever and ever. Amen" (D&C 88:133). This kind of fellowship explains why Latter-day Saints feel at home wherever they are when they meet other Latter-day Saints. Anyone moving to a new city or meeting another member of the church for the first time in a strange place, such as when on vacation, can experience instantly having a friend, instantly being at home. The saints have already come together in coming to Christ through baptism and the gift of the Holy Ghost, and any meeting they hold symbolizes and enacts that prior union. Our modern worship services are an obvious instance of this, but so are our more mundane meetings, from work on welfare projects, to chance meetings on vacation, to our first contact with the saints in cities or towns that are new to us. Paul would like to join with the saints in Rome, just as he would presumably enjoy visiting with saints in other places, but given his duty to preach the gospel of Christ, he will come to Rome only if the Father wills it.

JST Verse 10

Making request of you, to remember me in your prayers, I now write unto you, that you will ask him in faith, that if by any means //, at length, I may serve you with my labors, and may have a prosperous journey by the will of God, to come unto you.

The Greek and King James versions of verse 10 make Paul's request part of his prayer. Joseph Smith's version seems to make it a request Paul makes of the saints in Rome: "remember me in your prayers" and "ask him . . . if . . . I may serve you." Joseph Smith's version is problematic in that the

grammar is odd, but not impossible. The question is how to connect the prayer in verse 9 with the request in verse 10. The grammar of Joseph Smith's version suggests that Paul's request of the saints is part of his prayer: he prays that the saints will be kept and will remember him in their prayers.

However, if verse 9 were to end with a semicolon rather than a comma (this is entirely possible because early-nineteenth-century punctuation was anything but consistent and rule governed) and verse 10 were to begin with the word *and*, then the two verses together would easily make sense. The oddity of their relation would disappear. With that simple change of punctuation, the Joseph Smith Translation of verses 9 and 10 would read: "For God is my witness, whom I serve, that without ceasing I make mention of you always in my prayers, that you may be kept through the Spirit, in the gospel of his Son; and making request of you, to remember me in your prayers, I now write unto you, that you will ask him in faith, that if by any means, at length, I may serve you with my labors, and may have a prosperous journey by the will of God, to come unto you." If this revision is accurate, verse 9 would express Paul's prayer that the saints be kept in the gospel, and verse 10 would express his request that the saints pray for him to have a safe journey and to come to visit them.

Another difference between Joseph's translation and the standard text, the deletion of the word *now*, also changes the meaning. The King James Version says that Paul would like to visit Rome now, while Joseph Smith's revision of the verse says that Paul would like to visit Rome at some time in the future. This revision makes Paul's visit considerably more tentative. Since it is possible to read the Greek as implying only a general hope that Paul will visit the saints in Rome—perhaps the

> For I long to see you, that I may impart unto you some spiritual gift, to the end ye may be established; That is, that I may be comforted together with you by the mutual faith both of you and me.

visit he proposes will be accomplished only by the letter he is writing—Joseph Smith's changes are in line with one possible meaning of the Greek text.

Finally, the Prophet adds "I may serve you with my labors" to what the Romans should pray for. Not only should they pray that he can come to them, but also that he can serve them. This addition anticipates what we will see in verse 13 (see page 49), namely, Paul's hope that he can have fruit among the Romans. It also recalls the potentially provocative comparison of the Roman church members to the gentiles that we have already seen (see verse 5).

Verse 11

Long

The Greek word translated "long" (*epipotheo*, ἐπιποθέω) is a combination of a word meaning "to yearn or to long for something" and a prefix that intensifies the meaning of the word. One could read that Greek word as saying "to long for something especially."

Impart

Impart means "share with."

Spiritual

The gift Paul brings through his service in the spirit is a gift of the Spirit. The word *spirit* and the words related to it are rich. Quite literally, the Greek word for *spirit* (*pneuma*, πνεῦμα) means "breath" or "wind." (For more on *pneuma*, see page 42.) Because to be inhabited by a spirit is to be alive, and to be alive is, most obviously, to breathe, the connection be-

tween breath and spirit is not difficult to see or understand. In Hebrew, *spirit* and *breath* are similarly connected. Hebrew and Greek writers often use the literal meanings of the word *spirit* to connect ideas. For example, the breath of life breathed into Adam (see Genesis 2:7) and the Holy Spirit we receive when we are born again can be connected as parallels via the word *spirit*. Jesus' discussion with Nicodemus (see John 3:5–8) about spiritual rebirth uses the same connection to draw a parallel between physical birth and spiritual rebirth and to teach about the gift of the Holy Ghost and our inability to explain its inspiration.

Given the association in Greek between the word *spirit* and the breath of life, it is appropriate to see in Paul's reference to a spiritual gift a reference to the gift of life. Paul offers the Roman saints a gift that will give them life. If they were not already members of the church, he might be offering them the gift that comes through baptism, the gifts associated with being members of the church. But because he is specifically addressing baptized members, we must ask ourselves what further gift he could offer. I think we will see that he is offering them the gift of an understanding of sanctification: the gift that shows how God transforms what is unclean into what is clean, what is unholy into what is holy.

Gift

The gift Paul has may be this letter or it may be his apostolic visit. As mentioned on page 29, the Greek word translated "gift," *charisma* (χάρισμα), is a cognate of the word translated "grace" (*charis*, χάρις). Paul has received grace and has been called to deliver a message that reflects that grace. His message itself is a spiritual gift, or a grace, to the Roman saints. Paul wants to make it plain that his love and concern for the saints generates the message, and his message also reflects the

Father's loving-kindness toward them. If we recall the two parts of grace (see the discussion of verse 5, page 29), then the gift offered, which reflects the Father's loving-kindness, should be received with thanks and gratitude. Though Paul's letter is partly a call to repentance and might seem harsh to those who do not want to hear it, it is offered in kindness and should be received in gratitude. Doctrine and Covenants 121:41–46 tells us that a call to repentance must be made lovingly—with grace. Here we see that it should also be received with gratitude, for a call to repentance is a gift that can strengthen us if we accept it.

Established

The Greek word for *established* (*stērizō*, στηρίζω) means "set firmly in place," as well as "supported" and even "propped up."[69] (See its use in Romans 16:25, where it is translated "stablish.") Oddly, the verb is in the aorist case, meaning that it refers to a completed event or a specific point in time when something is or will be completed. Usually, but not necessarily, the aorist tense is used to refer to past events. Since Paul is not referring to something in the past, he uses the aorist case to say that he desires to give the Romans a spiritual gift so that, at a definite point in time, they will have been made firm. His prayer is not for something in general, but for specific support for the Romans, perhaps at the time of his intended visit.

To the end ye may be established

This letter is a way of supporting and establishing—strengthening—the members in Rome. In modern terms, it is a way of sustaining them, for to sustain is to support, establish, and strengthen. The spiritual gift that Paul longs to give them, an explanation of sanctification, is something that will strengthen and sustain them.

JST Verse 11

For I long to see you, that I may impart unto you some spiritual gift, <u>that it may be established in you</u> to the end / /;

In the Joseph Smith Translation, the purpose of Paul's letter is to make the spiritual gift Paul has to offer firm in the saints rather than to sustain them. The difference is one of emphasis rather than substance, because if the spiritual gift is strengthened in the saints, then they have also been strengthened.

However, Joseph's translation changes the meaning of this verse. The King James translation uses *end* as part of the phrase *to the end* (a phrase that is translated from one Greek word meaning "in order to"), but in Joseph's translation the phrase refers to the saints' duty to endure to the end. In the King James and Greek versions of this verse, *end* means "purpose." In the Joseph Smith Translation, it means "final point." The Prophet's understanding of the verse underscores the purpose of the letter: Paul wants to convert the saints in Rome—not only to the gospel itself, but also to the holy life the gospel demands of those who have accepted it. Paul wants to show the saints in Rome the difference between mere membership in the church and a saintly life that is in accordance with their calling.

Verse 12

Comfort

The word Paul uses for *comfort* is *sumparakaleō* (συμπαρακαλέω) and literally means "called together." As mentioned before (see page 10), it is a wordplay on *called* (see verses 1, 6, and 7). We usually think of comfort in terms of sympathy and thus think of comfort as a matter of consolation, reassurance, or soothing. That is not incorrect, but it is useful

> Now I would not have you ignorant, brethren, that oftentimes I purposed to come unto you, (but was let hitherto,) that I might have some fruit among you also, even as among other Gentiles.

to think of the word *comfort* etymologically. In Latin, *com* means "with" and *fort* is associated with strength (hence the English words *fort* and *fortitude*), so *comfort* means "to be strong with." This is the meaning of *comfort* in the King James translation and is also what the Greek word indicates. To be comforted is to be strengthened, and we are strengthened together and have strength with another. Offering consolation and reassurance is one way we can strengthen others, one way we can comfort them, but it is not the only way. Our way of thinking about the word *comfort* is narrower than was Paul's.

The phrase *comforted together* emphasizes being with one another; the Roman saints are called to be with each other by virtue of their membership in the church. *Encouraged* is a good synonym for *comforted together*, and its etymology is similar to that of *comfort*: "to give courage, hope, or confidence." This is at least one major sense in which the Holy Ghost is a comforter: besides giving sympathy, he strengthens and encourages by being with us in our trials. As the Second Comforter, the Savior will also stand with us (see page 10).

The preaching of the gospel that leads to repentance, the support that Paul will offer in this letter, brings comfort and hope—not just comfort against the ills and misfortunes of life and hope that we will have something better in the foreseeable future (though both certainly are included), but a general feeling of peace and comfort, the assurance that we are on the right track and acceptable to God even when we do not know what to expect, even

when we have no reason for natural hope (see Romans 4:18). Comfort, strength, and hope come not only through our faith in Christ as individuals, but also through our faith in and with one another. In the community of the church, faith in God founds and creates faith in one another, and faith in one another strengthens our faith in God. Bearing our testimonies to each other strengthens us all. Though we must each work out our own salvation, we do so together. Part of working out salvation is comforting one another, strengthening and encouraging one another through our faith, as Paul is doing here.

The mutual faith of both you and me

In the phrase *the mutual faith of both you and me*, Paul is not emphasizing his apostolic authority. Instead, he is emphasizing what the word *comfort* means: by being with the saints, serving them, and preaching to them, Paul will not only strengthen them through his faith, but he will be strengthened by their faith. His visit, whether physical or by letter, will bless them both. Anyone who, like Paul, has served in the spirit (see verse 9, pages 42–43) has had a similar experience.

Paul may also be explaining why he is coming to Rome, though his usual practice is to preach only where others have not (see Romans 15:20).

Notice that Paul does not speak of faith as an individual thing. We have an individualistic understanding of faith—his faith and my faith—but Paul speaks of the collective faith among the saints. To see this difference more clearly, compare Abraham with Achilles, the hero of Homer's *Iliad*. Achilles trusts only himself, and he claims all the credit: "*I* am going to get Hector." "*I* am going to possess the prize." In contrast, when commanded to sacrifice his son, Isaac, Abraham trusts Isaac (Isaac is probably in his thirties[70] and seems not to be a simple, mute victim), Isaac trusts Abraham, and they both trust God, who also obviously trusts them. Abraham is willing to give up everything, including all hope of having his divine promise fulfilled, simply because the Lord demands it. Achilles considers trust or faith in and with others to be secondary at best, but such faith and trust are at the very heart of Abraham's experience. The trust that we see among Abraham, Isaac, and God, as well as in Paul's letter, does not occur merely in the individual. It happens among the saints.

JST Verse 12

// That I may be comforted together with you by the mutual faith both of you and me.

The only difference between Joseph Smith's version of verse 12 and the King James Version is the deletion of the introductory phrase *that is*. If the phrase is included, verse 12 restates verse 11: giving the Roman saints a spiritual gift to sustain them is the same as their being comforted together by faith. By deleting the opening phrase, the Joseph Smith Translation makes this verse a consequence of verse 11: Paul wants to give the Romans a spiritual gift to strengthen the gospel in them so that he can be comforted together with the Romans by their mutual faith.

Verse 13

I would not have you ignorant

The phrase *I would not have you ignorant* is common in Paul's writing (see Romans 11:25; 1 Thessalonians 4:13; 1 Corinthians 10:1; 12:1; 2 Corinthians 1:8). Though the saints in Rome are renowned for their faith, they can still learn what it means to be saints. Paul writes to them for that reason. He believes that he can have a harvest from among them as he has had among the gentiles.

Brethren

The intimacy Paul shows with the word *brethren* may be surprising given that, though he knows some of the Roman saints personally (see Romans 16:3, 6–16), he is generally unacquainted with the Romans because he has never been to Rome. The intimacy is also a little odd considering the formality of the opening of the letter. On the other hand, an intimate feeling toward other members of the church, even those one does not know, is hardly unusual (see the discussion of *by the will of God* in verse 10, pages 44–45, as well as examples of Paul's similar intimacy in Romans 7:1, 4; 8:12; 10:1; 11:25; 15:14, 30; 16:17). Fitzmyer points out that speaking of the saints as brothers was adopted from Palestinian Jewish usage[71] (compare Deuteronomy 15:1–18 for the Jewish basis of that usage).

I purposed to come unto you

In the phrase *I purposed to come unto you*, the Greek word translated "purposed" indicates at least intention and probably a definite plan. On the other hand, as explained in the discussion of verse 10 (page 44), that plan may or may not have been to make a physical journey to Rome.

Was let hitherto

Let, in the phrase *was let hitherto*, does not mean "allowed," as we might expect. It means "prevented." We do not know what has kept Paul from coming to the Romans, whether by letter or in person, but when we consider this remark in conjunction with the statement in verse 10 that he has been praying that he might come, we can perhaps conclude that the Lord has until now refused permission. If that is the case, verse 13 may imply that Paul was previously prevented from coming because he would not have been able to find fruit among them. Perhaps their

> I am debtor both to the Greeks and the Barbarians; both to the wise, and to the unwise.

reputation for righteousness would earlier have prevented them from hearing Paul's message, but now they are ready.

Fruit

The metaphor of fruit is obvious. In Greek, the word *fruit* generally indicates the products of one's labor, what comes as a result of work.[72] Note that this metaphor questions some of our ordinary thinking about work, especially how we sometimes think about our work in the church. A tree does not produce fruit through an extraordinary effort. It produces fruit naturally. The fruit is the natural result of the tree's being what it is. One can hardly imagine admonishing an apple tree to try harder to produce better fruit. To produce better fruit, the apple tree must change itself, and that is almost surely impossible. Perhaps the tree must be pruned. Perhaps it must be fertilized. The apple tree can be worked on, but if it is to produce better fruit, it must be a better apple tree, and it cannot do this on its own.

That our works are compared to fruits should therefore give us pause, as should the fact that we are judged by those fruits. Just like an apple tree, we produce fruit—works—of one kind or another because we are human beings. There is no alternative; our fruits are the natural product of who we are. If we want better fruit, we must become better people. But, like the apple tree or the olive tree (see Jacob 5), we cannot make ourselves better. That is the work of the One who tends us.

If we are to be better, we must repent and make ourselves available to do God's work. We must submit to him as the tree submits to the farmer. Concentrating on the fruit we produce will not help. Comparing our fruit to that of others will probably be counterproductive. Gritting our teeth, cinching our belts, and firmly deciding to produce better fruit will not help. Neither will setting the goal of producing better fruit and writing it in our planners or imagining ourselves as better producers. Only becoming better people will do the job. But we cannot become better simply by choosing to be better. Becoming better is not really the result of an expenditure of our effort. A tree is a better tree because of the care given it by the gardener. Some trees may produce bad fruit in spite of that care, but they can hardly claim to have done so by an act of their will. Likewise, we may reject what the Father offers us through his Son and produce bad fruit. However, if we accept what is offered, we will be good and our fruit will be good, but that fruit will be nothing of which we can boast or be proud. Our fruit is not our work, but the Father's and the Son's (compare the discussion of *a servant of Jesus Christ* in verse 1 [pages 3–9] and the allegory of the olive tree in Jacob 5).

That I might have some fruit among you also, even as among other Gentiles

With the phrase *that I might have some fruit among you also, even as among other Gentiles*, Paul indicates that he would like a harvest among the Romans as he has had among others. In other words, he expects the saints in Rome to be better as a result of his service.

The Greek emphasizes the comparison of the Roman congregations to the other gentiles. Literally it reads, "Also among you, even as also among the other gentiles." The church in Rome may be primarily composed of gentiles—Greeks and Romans, rather than Jews. However, as is obvious from the content of the letter, there are a number of Jews among them (see the list of names in Romans 16, which includes Jewish, Roman, Greek, and

Latin names). Paul is writing to all the members of the church in Rome. He compares them to gentiles, perhaps because most are gentiles or perhaps because all are living in a gentile city. Paul uses the word *gentiles* in an equivocal way.

JST Verse 13

Now I would not have you ignorant, brethren, that oftentimes I purposed to come unto you, (but was <u>hindered</u> hitherto,) that I might have some fruit among you also, even as among other Gentiles.

The only change is one of clarification: *hindered* rather than *let*.

Verse 14

I am debtor

Why does Paul say he is indebted? After all, he is preaching and the Romans are receiving the gift he offers. It seems they should be indebted to him. However, in verse 12 Paul says that the saints and he will be strengthened if they can share their faith, and in verse 13 he mentions that he would like a harvest from among them. He seems, therefore, to be indebted on several counts. First, he has gathered fruit from among both the Greeks and the non-Greeks. That is in itself rewarding. It has often been noted that genuine service to another brings satisfaction. (And what greater service could there be than preaching the message of Christ?) Service also brings a sense of gratitude. When we serve others, the feeling that results is not pride, but thankfulness—thankfulness for the people we have served, for our relation to them, for the work we have done, for our Father in Heaven. Anyone who has helped another hear and understand the gospel and then seen that person accept it is familiar with this feeling.

Paul is indebted to all people because he is indebted to Christ. To be obligated to the

Savior is to be obligated to those for whom he died. In one sense, to owe is to be owned: I am owned by those whom I owe. Because Paul owes Jesus Christ, he also owes those for whom Jesus Christ has sacrificed. As a result, Paul is not only a slave of Christ, but also a slave of those to whom he preaches. He preaches to them because he owes it to them. Though Paul is an apostle, the saints and those to whom he has been called to preach are his masters.

Building on this notion, we can conclude that if, as verse 12 indicates, our faith is shared rather than individual, then we are indebted to each other. Having been purchased by the blood of Christ, each is owned by all others; each always owes the other as Paul owes him. We cannot escape our obligation to one another except by dying spiritually.

Paul's debt might well come as a surprise to many of his contemporaries in Rome, especially considering that they may think that he at times deals with them harshly. It is odd to imagine a slave owing his master a call to repentance, but that is exactly what Paul owes the saints. His obligation is to bring them grace and peace (see verse 7, pages 28–29). It is to do for them what they need—what the Father would do for them—not necessarily what they desire. If I were to attempt to meet such an obligation on the basis of only my own understanding, then I could never be sure that what I did, even if it were in accordance with the other's will, was what that person genuinely needed. Because I can be sure of neither the goodness of my will nor the will of another human being, I cannot deal fairly with others based on what either of us thinks is best. In other words, I cannot be sure of my own justice. In fact, the more sure I am of it, the more likely I am to be wrong about it. I must always worry that my justice is really injustice, but the Father is truly just. To the degree that my

> So, as much as in me is, I am ready to preach the gospel to you that are at Rome also.

service to my fellows is according to the will of the Father, rendered as part of my slavery to the Son, I need not worry about whether I have done right (though I must always be wary of being overly confident that my service is indeed what the Father wills). My will becomes irrelevant, and as a servant, my actions are not really mine. In this idea we see the necessity of being enslaved to God rather than having free will.

The theme of being indebted comes up again in chapters 3 and 4, where we see that even father Abraham is indebted and cannot claim sanctification as his right.

Greeks

The word *Greeks* refers to those who speak Greek. Though the Romans ruled the Mediterranean world and spoke Latin, Greek was the language of the cultured, even among the Romans. As a result, the word *Greek* was often used by people of the time to refer to the dominant culture.

Barbarians

Barbarians refers to those who do not speak Greek. In English the word *barbarian* refers to someone without culture. Although the Greek word *barbaros* (βάρβαρος; the Greeks thought the word mimicked the sound of non-Greek languages) can imply a lack of culture rather than only a difference of language, it does not necessarily do so, and it does not seem to carry that implication here. It is just the complement of *Greek*. Thus "the Greeks and the barbarians" includes everyone.

The wise

In Greek and Roman philosophical thought, the wise are those who know how to live well. They are those who have learned "the meaning of life." The overarching goal of Greek education was to achieve wisdom, and this goal had a great influence on Roman education. In its best form, Greek philosophy (literally "the love of wisdom" and therefore the name for education), which originated in Socrates' life and his quest for wisdom as virtue, centered on teaching us that we are unwise. The point of Greek and Roman philosophy and education was to gain wisdom (recall the discussion of Stoic wisdom on page 5).

The unwise

A better translation than "unwise" might be "foolish," though the word *unwise* is a good contrast to *wise*. Literally, the Greek word translated "unwise" (*anoētos*, ἀνόητος) means something like "mindless." Paul is using the terms *wise* and *unwise* only generally, but either term can also refer specifically to those who are converted or unrepentant. From the point of view of the world, the converted are foolish and those who seek their own self-interest rather than the glory of God are wise. The reverse is true from God's point of view (see 1 Corinthians 1:25; 3:19; 2 Nephi 9:42).

As is true of much of what follows in the letter to the Romans, what Paul says in verse 14 would have been a scandal to educated Greeks and Romans. As we have seen, the whole point of Greek and Roman philosophy was wisdom, or the overcoming of ignorance, and it would thus be difficult and even scandalous for a philosopher of Paul's time to have thought himself indebted to the unwise.

Both to Greeks, and to the Barbarians; both to the wise, and to the unwise

The phrases *both to the Greeks, and to the Barbarians* and *both to the wise, and to the unwise* indicate that Paul is indebted to everyone. The words *Greeks* and *barbarians* emphasize language and culture, and the words *wise* and *unwise* emphasize mental ability or understanding within the culture. Paul divides everyone in two ways. These two ways overlap each other but are also distinct, and they emphasize that Paul is indebted to all: the Greeks and the non-Greeks and everyone within either group.

The King James translation expands what is quite terse in the Greek version of verse 14. Quite literally, the Greek reads, "Greeks and Romans, wise and unwise," with the word *to* implied in each case by the grammatical form of the nouns.

JST Verse 14

No change.

Verse 15

So

The word *so* indicates that what follows is the consequence of Paul's indebtedness. He is ready to preach the gospel to the Romans because he owes it to them.

As much as in me is

In the phrase *as much as in me is*, Paul shows his humility by acknowledging that he has limitations.

I am ready to preach the gospel to you that are at Rome also

With the phrase *I am ready to preach the gospel to you that are at Rome also*, the KJV indicates that Paul is ready to preach the gospel. The Greek indicates that he is not just ready, but eager. This implies that the Roman saints need to have the gospel preached to them—in spite of their reputation for faithfulness. Given what Paul has already said about their faithfulness, the Roman saints might be offended that he wants to preach the gospel to them as he has among others, most of whom were unbelievers. It might be especially offen-

sive to those who are renowned for their faithfulness to be told that Paul hopes his preaching will find fruit among them as it has among the unbelievers, but Paul has already made clear that his letter is to strengthen, not to offend. Perhaps he has built up to this point slowly so that they will not easily be offended. Perhaps that is why he has prefaced this letter by pointing out his understanding of them and his love for them. In fact, to their credit, he thinks they are ready for his message of repentance, a message intended specifically for those renowned for faithfulness.

JST Verse 15

<u>And</u>, as much as in me is, I am ready to preach the gospel to you that are at Rome also.

The King James translation begins verse 15 with *so*, a word that implies that verse 15 describes a consequence of verse 14. This is a reasonable interpretation of the Greek text. The editors of the Greek manuscript have put a semicolon at the end of verse 14 to connect it to verse 15. It also seems reasonable to conclude that verses 13 and 14 are two descriptions of a single fact: Paul desires to have fruit among the Romans, and he is indebted to all. Thus, as traditionally rendered, verses 13 and 14 indicate that Paul wants those in Rome to know that he has intended to come to them in order to find fruit among all people. Verse 15 then tells us that Paul is ready to preach the gospel in Rome because he intends to have fruit among the Roman saints and is indebted to all.

In contrast, Joseph Smith's version of verse 15 is parallel to verse 14 rather than a consequence of it. This elevates the importance of verse 15. Joseph Smith's version indicates that Paul wants the church members in Rome to know two independent things: (1) he has intended to come to them, and (2) he is ready to do so.

VERSES 16–17

King James

₁₆For I am not ashamed of the gospel of Christ: for it is the power of God unto salvation to every one that believeth; to the Jew first, and also to the Greek. ₁₇For therein is the righteousness of God revealed from faith to faith: as it is written, The just shall live by faith.

Alternate

₁₆I am not ashamed of the gospel; for it is God's power to bring salvation for all those who are trusting, to the Jew first and to the Greek. ₁₇For through trust, God's justice is revealed by the gospel to those who trust, even as it has been written: "And the just will live by trust."

Verse 16

The first part of verse 16, Paul's statement that he is not ashamed of the gospel, provides a conclusion to his lengthy greeting. The second part of the verse acts as a transition to the theme of the letter (stated in verse 17), explaining why Paul is not ashamed of the gospel and setting up the discussion of the saving power of faith.

I am not ashamed

In the phrase *I am not ashamed*, Paul uses the rhetorical device litotes (understatement) to declare that he is proud of the gospel. If he

were afraid to preach repentance to both the saints and those not yet converted, he would not be proud of the gospel. Though Roman intellectuals of his day considered the gospel common or low class—a laughing matter at best—and though it was a stumbling block to the Jews, it does not put Paul to shame. He trusts in the gospel and its message of hope for sinners. Thus, though Paul was himself guilty of assenting to and assisting in killing one of the Seventy (see Acts 7:58; 8:1), now that he trusts in the gospel and understands and accepts Christ's redemption and what it requires of him, he is not ashamed to preach.

> For I am not ashamed of the gospel of Christ: for it is the power of God unto salvation to every one that believeth; to the Jew first, and also to the Greek.

Of the gospel

Paul earlier emphasized the preaching of the gospel rather than its content (see the discussion of verse 1, pages 13–14). When Paul says he is not ashamed of the gospel, he says that he is happy and proud to preach the gospel.

It is the power of God unto salvation

The gospel is not just information that people can judge objectively and then decide whether they will accept or reject it. The gospel is not just a message, but power. Thus, to hear the gospel preached is to be affected, and the effect of preaching is salvation. Recall verse 4, which says that Jesus was "declared to be the Son of God with power." The Father makes that declaration not only through the resurrection, but also through the preaching of his servants.

Like other New Testament writers, Paul takes the saving power of gospel preaching quite literally (again, see the discussion of *gospel* in verse 1, pages 13–14). When done by the Spirit, the preaching of the gospel is the power that brings salvation to all who will hear. This is why Paul has no shame when he preaches: through his preaching, those who, like him, are guilty of sin can receive salvation from their sins. Paul needs no confidence in his own intellect or training because he has confidence in the power of the gospel. In fact, not to have that confidence in the gospel would be to be ashamed of it. When we doubt our ability to do the Lord's work, we really doubt that work itself and we doubt the Lord's ability to do his work through us.

The scriptures, especially the Book of Mormon, are full of evidence that Paul correctly says that "faith cometh by hearing, and hearing by the word of God" (Romans 10:17). This belief motivates the letter to the Romans and Paul's other letters. Clearly, the missionaries in the Book of Mormon teach with power and can convert in dramatic ways because they preach the gospel. For example, Ammon converts Lamoni simply through preaching the gospel (see Alma 18–19), and the remarkable sermons of King Benjamin and Alma converted many (see Mosiah 1–4; Alma 5). As Alma reminds us, the preaching of the word tends to have a more powerful effect on people than even the sword (see Alma 31:5).

The King James translation indicates that preaching the gospel is "the power of God unto salvation." However, the Greek has no definite article. Thus the alternate translation is "it is God's power."

In Paul's time, the gospel was believed and taught by only a small group and seemed to have little impact on the world. Few knew anything about it. It might, therefore, have been tempting to think of the gospel as a powerless and ineffectual thing, especially when compared to the power and influence of the Roman government, which many in Rome, including the Roman saints, probably identified with. But Paul does not share that identification with the Roman government or the feeling that the gospel is weak. He understands that exactly the opposite is true: the Roman government, like any human government, is ultimately powerless and ineffectual, and only the gospel has the power necessary for salvation.

Salvation

The Greek word *sōtērion* (σωτήριον) means "rescue from evil or harm." In Judaism, Yahweh delivers, or saves, Israel (see Isaiah 45:17; the Septuagint uses the verb form of *sōtērion*).

Paul explicitly identifies Jesus and Yahweh as he does in verse 3.

The Greek word *sōtērion* derives from a word meaning "safe and sound."[73] "Safe" indicates that we are free from harm; "sound," that we are healthy, without flaw. Paul uses *sōtērion* only in connection with salvation from spiritual death. Those who receive salvation are made safe from the adversary, and their shortcomings, spiritual and physical, are removed. The obvious implication is that when we are not yet saved, we are neither safe nor healthy spiritually. If the world and Satan are our masters, then we are always in danger of physical and spiritual death, and we are always diseased, no matter the state of our bodies.

Believeth

Here, the Greek word *pisteuō* (πιστεύω), translated "believeth," is a verbal form of the word *pistis* (πίστις), translated "faith" or "trust" in other places (see, for example, verse 17 and the discussion of *faith* in verse 5, page 31). Connecting this word to other places where the Greek uses *pistis* by using a variation of one English word in each place would help us better understand Paul's message. *Pisteuō* might therefore be better translated as "is faithful" or "trusts." As mentioned earlier, it is important to remember the connection between faith and trust as we read Romans. *Believeth* does not make that connection. It is also not an active enough word; it is too passive for what Paul describes in verse 16. The gospel message is the power of salvation for the faithful; in other words, it is the power of salvation for those who trust God.

We can use the word *belief* to describe our response to the gospel message. However, if by *belief* we mean merely "assent to the truth of a proposition" (this is not usually how the scriptures use the word), then belief is not sufficient to salvation. Trust—that is, faith—involves considerably more. If we have trust we also have belief, for we agree that what we trust in is true and we believe what we are told by the one we trust. However, the reverse is not true. We can believe something to be true without putting our trust in the person who told us and even without putting our trust in what we believe to be true, though the latter is inexplicable. Satan seems to do just that. He and his cohorts believe that Christ is the Savior—they even know that he is—but they trust only themselves and act against their belief (see James 2:19).

We must exercise faith to be saved. Our faith is already a response to a power, not just to a message. We can exercise faith or reject the power of the gospel, but whichever we do, we are responding to what God has initiated. That is how the Christ is the "author and finisher of our faith" (Hebrews 12:2). He is the author in that he initiated the plan of salvation, making faith possible. He is the origin of our faith in that he created a world, including us, and he created a message that cannot be ignored. To hear the message is to respond to it, whether positively or negatively. He also created us to be open to the message, able to hear and respond to it (for more about this, see verse 20, pages 78–81; 2 Nephi 32:9 suggests something similar). Faith is the natural consequence of hearing the message of the gospel, and the gospel message is the power of salvation to those who respond to it in faith. A surprising result of this understanding of faith is that only our refusal to obey the message can be said to be our own act (see the earlier discussion of freedom in verse 1, pages 3–9). Christ is the finisher of our faith in that he makes possible the perfection of our faith (see the earlier discussion of perfection, pages 21–22; see also Moroni 6:4).

> For therein is the righteousness of God revealed from faith to faith: as it is written, The just shall live by faith.

To the Jew first, and also to the Greek

Here *Greek* means "non-Jew." One understanding of the phrase *to the Jew first, and also to the Greek* notes that this is the order in which the gospel was preached. Paul believes that the Jews have first claim on the word of God (see Romans 9–11), but this seems to involve a paradox. On the one hand, everyone is absolutely equal before God (see Romans 3:22; 10:12), and as Paul has just mentioned in verse 16, all who are faithful can receive salvation. On the other hand, the Jews have first claim to receiving the gospel. Is there any way to account for this apparent contradiction? One way is to remember what it means to be chosen. To be chosen is to be set apart (see the discussion of *saints* in verse 7, pages 34–36). Something chosen is an instrument for a holy purpose; it is something God uses to bring about his purposes. The chosen people, therefore, are a people chosen for a particular work. They are holy people because they are chosen, not because the are necessarily any more pure or more privileged than anyone else. In fact, one could argue that it would be a mistake to choose the most righteous people to represent the other peoples of the earth, because saving such a people would not sufficiently demonstrate God's power to save from sin. But what might such an argument say about the latter-day chosen people? The Jews received the gospel first, not because they were privileged, but because they were the instrument God chose to use in working out the salvation that is available to all equally. Presumably our case as the latter-day chosen people is similar: we ought not to think of ourselves as chosen because of our righteousness, but chosen for a work. Like the Jews of old, we are to be a light to the gentiles, that is, to do the work of lighting the world. It does not follow that we are that light because we are holy. As such scriptures as 3 Nephi 11:11; 12:16; and 18:24 make clear, we are a light only insofar as the light of Jesus Christ shines in us, only insofar as we show his light in the world.

JST Verse 16

No change.

Verse 17

Verse 17 is the thesis of the letter: God's righteousness is revealed in the gospel "from faith to faith." In verse 16 Paul said that the gospel is the power of God to salvation. Recall that by *gospel* he means something active, the faithful preaching and living of the gospel, not just a list of doctrines or the recitation of such a list. In verse 17 Paul will show at least part of what the gospel entails—how the power of God is salvation for those who are faithful—by concentrating on the role faith and trust play in the plan of salvation.

For therein

For therein means "because in the gospel." One reason Paul is not ashamed is that the gospel, the message of the atonement, reveals God's righteousness.

The righteousness of God

The verb *dikaioō* (δικαιόω), the root of the word that the KJV translates as "righteousness" (*dikaiosunē*, δικαιοσύνη) in the phrase *the righteousness of God*, means "to declare something to be just" as well as "to do right." The word *dikaiosunē* could also be translated "justice."[74] In fact, "justice" might be a more helpful translation than "righteousness" for our purposes. However, as we will see, it is important not to assume that justice and mercy are at odds with each other. To speak of God's righteousness, as Paul does here, is not to speak of the opposite of his mercy. In fact, it is to do anything but that.

The phrase *the righteousness of God* is grammatically ambiguous, and much of the dispute over how to understand Romans can be encapsulated in that ambiguity. It could mean "the righteousness characteristic of God," but it could also mean "the righteousness that originates from God."

Though the scriptures frequently speak of God's righteousness, this particular phrase is not used in the Septuagint, so there is no text to which we can compare this phrase to decide how to disambiguate it. Some readers (especially Protestants) believe that Paul means "the righteousness that originates from God."[75] They cite as evidence such passages as 1 Corinthians 1:30 and Philippians 3:9, where the genitive (the grammatical form translated "of" in English) clearly indicates origin, as well as Romans 5:17, where righteousness is spoken of as a gift, and Romans 10:3, which can plausibly be read as using the same phrase—*the righteousness of God*—to speak of the righteousness that has its origin in God.

On the other hand, there seems to be no such possibility in the Old Testament, where justice and mercy are both attributes of God and neither is in conflict with the other. God's exercising of justice, his defense of Israel, indeed is his mercy. In the Old Testament, God's righteousness is clearly spoken of as a divine attribute and never as a gift that he gives his children. Phrases referring to God's righteousness (e.g., Isaiah 41:10; 56:1; Psalms 5:8; 6–71; 2 Nephi 4:32–33) almost always mean his ability to defend his people against their enemies. As we have already seen, Paul is dependent on the Old Testament and its understanding of words and concepts (see,

for example, the discussion of *saints* in verse 7, pages 34–36). Without referring to the Old Testament, we will not understand much of what Paul says. The quotation in the second half of verse 17 is from Habakkuk 2:4, which clearly attributes righteousness to God as a characteristic. Thus there are good scriptural reasons to believe that the phrase should be translated "the righteousness that is characteristic of God."[76]

In the Old Testament, *righteousness* means "fidelity to covenants." The Father's righteousness is shown by his fidelity to his covenant with Israel. Israel will show her fidelity when she is faithful to her covenant: an individual is righteous by being faithful to the covenant, in other words by obeying the Law. It seems, therefore, that either Paul is introducing a new concept (the gift of righteousness), as Protestants often argue, or we should understand the phrase *the righteousness of God* as the Old Testament understands it (as referring to the righteousness characteristic of God).

There are good reasons for accepting either of these alternatives. We seem to be caught in an interpretive dilemma. However, this is a dilemma only if we insist that the two alternatives are mutually exclusive, if we insist that Paul is either introducing a new understanding or relying on Old Testament usage, but not both. Since both options are plausible and equally informative, I believe we should accept them both. Using Old Testament concepts and understanding, Paul shows us how the Father is righteous and merciful at the same time. He will later show us how the Divine fulfills his covenant obligation to us at the same time that he acts mercifully toward us. However, he will insist that neither of these actions is the result of a legalistic claim that we have on him as creditors to whom he owes salvation and exaltation. Thus Paul teaches something that his contemporaries in

> For therein is the righteousness of God revealed from faith to faith: as it is written, The just shall live by faith.

Judah did not understand, and he does so by expanding and clarifying the Old Testament concept of God's righteousness, namely, his ability to save his people. He introduces a new understanding of an ancient idea (we also find this idea in the Book of Mormon) rather than a completely new idea.

But what is this righteousness that the Lord gives as a gift and that is characteristic of him? The Greek word for *righteousness* (*dikaiosune*, δικαιοσύνη) comes from a word that originally meant "what is customary" and later came to have juridical significance as a term meaning "lawful" and "fair," as well as "precise," "exact," and "fit for use."[77] Its use among the Greeks was mostly ethical and legal. In the Septuagint, *dikaiosune* and its etymological relatives (such as its root, *dikaioo* [δικαιόω]) are used to translate a group of related Hebrew words meaning "holy" (those with the root צדק, *tsdq*). In turn, those Hebrew words have as their basic meaning "complying to a norm" and "fulfilling obligations or covenants." As mentioned, in the Old Testament, righteousness is most obviously a matter of fulfilling covenants and meeting obligations. Though there are similarities in meaning between the Greek and Hebrew groups of words, they are not identical. The Hebrew words have more to do with obligation and covenant, while the Greek words refer more to one's conformity to expectations. We will see that in using the Greek word, Paul carries Greek connotations into his work, but we will also see that the Hebrew meaning of *righteousness* is at least as important as the Greek meaning in Paul's thinking and understanding.

First let us consider this Greek word *dikaiosune* (δικαιοσύνη) and its Greek connotations. As noted earlier, another reasonable translation of the word is "justice." Such a translation recommends itself for the alternate translation because it prepares us for the quotation from Habakkuk that follows: "the just shall live by faith," or as Fitzmyer translates the clause, "the one who is upright shall find life through faith."[78] We often think of justice as sternly meting out deserved punishment. Or, at best, we think of it as giving what we owe to another. In keeping with one important Greek understanding of justice, we think of justice and fairness as equivalents. Closely related to this meaning is another meaning, "correct judgment," the ability to discriminate between good and evil and to act accordingly. On that reading of this verse, "the righteousness of God" refers to God's perfect ability to know good from evil and his perfect ability to act in accordance with that knowledge.

The story of Adam and Eve teaches us that the ability to judge between good and evil and to act on that judgment is what makes humans godlike (see Genesis 3:22; Moses 4:28). As Paul points out in verses 19–23, those whom God condemns as sinners are sinners because they exercise poor judgment. In other words, their unrighteousness is their injustice because they do not judge according to God's judgment (i.e., justice) but substitute their own for it. God is righteous because he judges correctly in fulfilling his covenants; they are unrighteous because they do not.

However, I think that in this passage *dikaiosune* indicates more than God's fairness and careful discrimination between good and evil, though obviously it must also include that. After all, Paul devotes a large portion of his letter to showing how the Father will save us even though we do not deserve salvation. God will be more than fair with us. A meaning of *dikaiosune* that is more in keeping with

Paul's message might be "God's ability to right wrongs." Sinners do not right wrongs, they commit them. The gospel is the revelation of God's justice, his ability to right wrongs. Even more than it is his correct judgment, the Father's righteousness is his ability to declare accurately that we are just or unjust and to change our state from unjust to just. It is his ability to right our wrongs. Not only can we trust him to be fair with us and not only can he discriminate accurately between good and evil, but he can also right the wrongs that come before him. In the context of covenants, the ability to judge right and wrong and to right wrongs is the ability to know who is and who is not in the covenant relation and to bring those who have fallen from the covenant relation back into it.

Consider next the connotations of the word *dikaiosunē* that come from its connection to Old Testament ideas, particularly the idea of covenant. Given Paul's rabbinic training, these covenantal connotations may be the most important for us to consider. As we have seen, in the Old Testament, righteousness and justice relate to obligation and covenant. Righteousness is meeting our obligations to the covenant of God, and this means obedience to law—specifically the law of Moses. In the Hebrew view, the law is not a set of human conventions for treating each other fairly (though such conventions might be an important consequence). For the Jews the law is the expression of a covenant with God; it is the expression of an obligation to God.[79] Those who are faithful to the law are justified—or made right—by God. Thus, according to the Old Testament, human justice is a matter of faithfulness and obedience rather than fairness. To be just is to live according to the will of God, in other words, in obedience to the law. Given what we have already seen in the discussion of *a servant of Jesus Christ* in verse

1, pages 3–9, to be just is to be a slave of God and to meet the obligations of one's servitude.

Though such an idea stretches our understanding of righteousness and justice because we often equate justice with fairness, it is important to notice that fairness is not obligatory in either the Old Testament or the New. Achieving fairness is not the point of the Hebrew law, because more than fairness is required. Consider Exodus 22:21–27:

> Thou shalt neither vex a stranger, nor oppress him: for ye were strangers in the land of Egypt. Ye shall not afflict any widow, or fatherless child. . . . If thou lend money to any of my people that is poor by thee, thou shalt not be to him as an usurer, neither shalt thou lay upon him usury. If thou at all take thy neighbour's raiment to pledge, thou shalt deliver it unto him by that the sun goeth down: For that is his covering only, it is his raiment for his skin: wherein shall he sleep? and it shall come to pass, when he crieth unto me, that I will hear; for I am gracious.

Similarly, James says, "Pure and unpolluted religion before God and the Father is this: to visit orphans and widows in their affliction, to keep oneself unspotted from the world" (James 1:27; author's translation). Neither of these scriptures requires us to treat others fairly. Both require that we do more than is fair, giving to others without regard to the question of what is fair to us.

The connection of the law with the covenant on one hand and justice on the other is evident in James's writing. I take it that the phrase *pure and unpolluted* implicitly refers to ritual cleanliness. The implication is that keeping oneself unspotted from the world, keeping the divine covenant, is a matter of meeting the ethical demand of orphans and widows, the types for all who come before us.

We might say that justice means rendering each his due, but the gospel teaches that

> For therein is the righteousness of God revealed from faith to faith: as it is written, The just shall live by faith.

such justice is different than God's. God renders salvation to those who trust in him rather than those to whom he owes it. In turn, both the Old Testament and the New Testament insist that obedience to the will of God—our justice—necessitates a new sense of rendering everyone their due: not what they deserve, but what they need. Justice is the ethical obligation of service to God and to our fellows.

The Savior made it clear that in the gospel, justice is not a matter of fairness or one's rights:

> And if any man will sue thee at the law, and take away thy coat, let him have thy cloke also. And whosoever shall compel thee to go a mile, go with him twain. Give to him that asketh thee, and from him that would borrow of thee turn not thou away. Ye have heard that it hath been said, Thou shalt love thy neighbour, and hate thine enemy. But I say unto you, Love your enemies, bless them that curse you, do good to them that hate you, and pray for them which despitefully use you, and persecute you; That ye may be the children of your Father which is in heaven: for he maketh his sun to rise on the evil and on the good, and sendeth rain on the just and on the unjust. (Matthew 5:40–45)

Our concept of fairness dictates none of what here describes Christian justice: if you lose a lawsuit, pay twice what is demanded; if a Roman soldier forces you to carry his equipment one mile (something that is probably itself unfair), go two; and bless those who curse you, returning good for evil. None of these acts would balance the scales of fairness, but

in doing them we imitate our Father in Heaven. His justice is characterized not by fairness and equality of exchange, but by service to those who are in need, even when that service is not fair, not equitable, not deserved. Fairness demands that we be treated in the same way that we treat others. However, if the Father were to treat us "fairly," we would be condemned because we have been unjust.[80] Instead, the Father gives us all that he has: "And he that receiveth my Father receiveth my Father's kingdom; therefore all that my Father hath shall be given unto him" (D&C 84:38; see 38:39). If we are to be just, we must imitate our just Father. We must give all that we have: "So likewise, whosoever he be of you that forsaketh not all that he hath, he cannot be my disciple" (Luke 14:33). God's justice is his consecration of everything he has to us. Similarly, for us to be just we must consecrate all that we have to divine service, a service that necessarily includes service to the poor, the widowed, the fatherless, and even our enemies. It turns out that the Greeks were right: justice is giving what we owe. However, we owe more than we might suspect if we think in terms of fairness and equity, for we owe everything.

Because we think of justice in terms of fairness and mercy in terms of going beyond fairness, we often conceive of justice and mercy as antithetical. However, an implication of the understanding of justice outlined above is that the scriptural description of God's righteousness shows no real difference between justice and mercy. For ancient prophets and apostles, one cannot be just without being merciful.

To this point the discussion may seem to have focused on the idea that the phrase *the righteousness of God* means "the righteousness that comes from God" rather than "the righteousness characteristic of God," even though

I have suggested that we cannot and should not decide between the two possible meanings of the phrase. That seeming focus is partly because it is so important to understand what righteousness means to us. However, to speak of the righteousness of God is to speak not only of the fact that God has made it possible for us to fulfill our covenantal obligations, it is also to speak of the fulfillment of his divine obligation.

Such an idea is bothersome to many. Traditionally, many Christians have been loath to ascribe obligation to God. In fact, one of Paul's major points is that we cannot obligate God by our obedience, because to do so would be to leave our positions as slaves. It would be to make God a debtor to us (see especially Romans 4). However, Jews have not been afraid to see the Divine as obligated to humans. Old Testament prophets called on God to fulfil his obligation to his people. In fact, in verse 17 Paul quotes from Habakkuk 2:4, where the Lord replies to such a remonstration (see page 65). In Habakkuk 1, the prophet Habakkuk remonstrates the Lord for not fulfilling his covenantal obligation to protect Israel from her enemies. The tradition of the righteous person who remonstrates with the Divine is an important element of many Jewish traditions.[81] Such remonstration is also not alien to our own religious tradition and experience (see D&C 121:1–6).

However, that the Divine is not obligated by our obedience does not mean he is not obligated to us at all. He is, in fact, obligated by his word, by his covenant. That is what I understand the Lord to mean when he says that he is bound when we do what he says (see D&C 82:10). For one thing, any reasonable notion of covenant implies obligation. By definition, if the Lord enters into a covenant, he is obliged in some way. Also, the Creator is obligated to his creatures as the parent to the child.

This obligation is equally unearned by the creature or child, but it is nevertheless very real.

One could argue, in fact, that the notion of grace (or loving-kindness) implies not only the absence of earned reward, but also the notion of moral obligation on the part of the one who offers grace. Without the moral obligation of parent to child and the obligation that comes with being a covenantor, any gift given by God would be merely arbitrary. It would not be a demonstration of his justice and righteousness, of his love. If to love someone is to be obligated to that person (though not necessarily by that person) and God loves us, then he is, in a very real sense, obligated to—but not by—us.

Revealed

Literally, the Greek word *apokaluptō* (ἀποκαλύπτω), translated "revealed," means "to unveil or uncover" and thus "to disclose" or "to reveal." Something of God's character, namely, his righteousness, is revealed in the power of the gospel. As we will see in verse 18 (pages 72–75), Paul is setting up a contrast. He will compare the way in which God's righteousness and justice is revealed with the way in which the unrighteousness and injustice of the sinful is revealed.

From faith to faith

The phrase *from faith to faith* is difficult to understand. Does it connect grammatically with *righteousness* or with *is the righteousness of God revealed*? Those who believe that the phrase *the righteousness of God* means "the righteousness that God gives" believe that *from faith to faith* modifies *righteousness*.[82] If this is true, the latter phrase tells us that the gift of righteousness springs from faith. On the other hand, those who believe that *righteousness* means "the righteousness that characterizes God" believe that *from faith to faith*

> For therein is the righteousness of God revealed from faith to faith: as it is written, The just shall live by faith.

modifies *is the righteousness of God revealed*, indicating that divine righteousness is revealed to us in our faith. Grammatically, it is difficult to justify the first possibility. To read this phrase as connecting to *righteousness* requires us to strain the plain grammatical sense and seems motivated solely by doctrinal considerations. I think it most reasonable to believe that *from faith to faith* explains how the revelation of divine righteousness occurs: if we exercise faith, we will come to see the righteousness of God.

The question of how this phrase connects to the rest of the sentence is easier to answer than is the question of what the phrase means. It can and has been taken to mean many things. For example, some read the phrase to mean "the righteousness that is revealed through preaching to hearers."[83] Along the same lines, others take it to mean "through divine faithfulness to human beings who are faithful."[84] Perhaps the phrase has no special meaning at all and is simply a way of emphatically making the point that faith is necessary.

Though the possibility that Paul is making a simple rhetorical gesture is strong, I think it even more likely that he is making a meaningful point by repetition, primarily because the rhetorical gesture is an unusual one. The best way to understand this phrase is to look at it one piece at a time. Consider the clause *is the righteousness of God revealed from faith*. The Greek word *ek* (ἐκ) is often accurately translated "from," as in the King James translation. Here, however, I think it is better understood as indicating instrumentality: "God's righteousness is revealed *by* faith." Paul's quotation of the last part of Habakkuk 2:4 at the end of this verse strongly suggests

that the instrumental reading of *ek* is correct, because the Septuagint version of Habakkuk 2:4 clearly uses *ek* instrumentally. Such a reading makes perfectly good sense however we decide to read the phrase *God's righteousness*. If the phrase refers to a characteristic of God, then we come to know that characteristic through our faith: as we trust him, we learn that he is just. If we read it as indicating the origin of human righteousness, then it says that human righteousness is accomplished by faith in the Divine. In this case, the instrumental reading of *ek* is most plausible: "by means of faith to faith" or "getting faith by means of faith."

The second element of the phrase *from faith to faith* is also reasonably easy to understand when considered by itself in the clause *is the righteousness of God revealed from faith to faith*. As we have seen, this clause can mean "the revelation of God's righteousness produces faith," interpreting the word *to* (Greek *eis*, εἰς) to indicate result rather than direction. But it may also be that Paul is using metonymy (substituting one word for another word or phrase with which it is easily associated). Perhaps Paul is substituting *faith* for *those who are faithful*." Verse 18 suggests that this is the best way to read this phrase, for it is conceptually parallel to verse 17 and suggests that wrath is revealed to the unrighteous through their unrighteousness.

Putting these ideas together, we can read the clause to mean "God's righteousness is revealed to the faithful by means of their faith." It could also mean "the revelation of God's righteousness produces faith by means of faith." The second of these two possibilities may seem dubious. The claim that God's righteousness is revealed by our faith may seem to be a vicious circle: we cannot know God's righteousness without already having faith, but without knowing that righteousness, how can we come to trust in God? Alma 32 is helpful here. Alma explains that our faith increases because we come to understand the revelation of the gospel. Thus progression is from faith to faith rather than from absence of faith to the acquisition of faith. We cannot claim to have come even to our faith on our own; it is a gift, something everyone has been given. For example, Alma does not say that *we* should plant a seed in our hearts and then see whether it grows, in spite of what is often said about the second half of his sermon. Rather, Alma says that a person should "give place, that a seed *may be planted* in your heart" (Alma 32:28). In other words, we should allow the seed to be planted. In fact, in Alma 33, the people send to Alma because they want to know how they can plant the seed. His answer: listen to the prophets (see Alma 33:3–17) and look to Christ (see Alma 33:19–22). In other words, plant the seed by letting it be planted, by hearing the prophets, and by having Christ as a standard and goal (see also scriptures such as 1 Corinthians 12:8–9; James 1:17; and the earlier discussion of *gospel* in verse 1, pages 13–14).

Comparison to Old Testament uses of the same grammatical structure lend support to two other interpretations of Paul's phrase. The Septuagint version of 1 Samuel 2:19 and 1 Chronicles 16:23 uses the same Greek grammatical structure in a phrase translated "from year to year," "from time to time," or "from day to day." This suggests that the phrase *from faith to faith* can be understood temporally. According to one such interpretation, the phrase means that God's righteousness is revealed from the faith of those before Christ to the faithful who live after Christ. In that case, it may by extension refer to a transition from the faith required by the Mosaic law to the faith required by the gospel, a transition revealed in divine righteousness, in other

words, in the offer of the Son. Or, still taken temporally, the phrase may tell us that God's justice has been revealed to the faithful in all times and in all places. According to another interpretation, if we compare this phrase to Psalm 84:7 ("from strength to strength," another grammatical parallel in the Septuagint), it may suggest a growth from less faith to more, so that the verse as a whole indicates that divine righteousness will be revealed in a growing faith.

As it is written

Paul is about to quote from Habakkuk 2:4. The phrase *as it is written* is the standard way of introducing citations of scripture. Ancient writers did not have footnoting systems or other ways of making citations, so they indicated that they were quoting scripture by beginning their quotations with this phrase.

Paul is not quoting from the version of the Old Testament on which our King James translation is based. The King James translation of the Old Testament is based on a Hebrew version of the Old Testament compiled between the seventh and tenth centuries A.D. and known as the Masoretic text. Paul may be using the Septuagint, a Greek translation of the Hebrew Old Testament made in about the third century B.C. (See page 4 for more on the Septuagint. The Septuagint is not necessarily better than the King James or the more recent reconstructions just because it is older.) However, Paul, does not quote exactly from the Septuagint as we have it. The Septuagint reads, "the just will live by my faith," which may mean either "the just will live because of God's faithfulness" or "the just will live because of his faith in me." Given the difference between Paul's quotation and the Septuagint, he may be using still another version of Habakkuk. There appear to have been no particular "authorized" versions of the books of

> For therein is the righteousness of God re-
> vealed from faith to faith: as it is written, The
> just shall live by faith.

the Old Testament at the time, perhaps because heresy was not yet a major problem.
Because the people of Paul's time did not
have to worry about which version of scripture was authoritative, they seem not to have
worried much about the differences between
various manuscripts. Except for the five
books of Moses (also called the Torah, including Genesis, Exodus, Leviticus, Numbers, and
Deuteronomy), books of scripture usually existed as separate volumes, and many existed
in more than one version. There was only
general agreement about what books were
part of the scriptural canon. All the books we
recognize were accepted as scripture, but
there were other books that many, including
Paul, also accepted, such as Wisdom (see
page 17). Though Paul uses the Septuagint
most frequently, he also appears to use other
versions as they suit his purposes. As a result,
sometimes the scriptures Paul quotes differ
from the version we find in the King James
translation.

On the other hand and perhaps even
more likely, the difference between Paul's
quotation and the Septuagint may be because
Paul is paraphrasing the scripture rather than
quoting it exactly.

Just

The Greek word for *just* (*dikaios*, δίκαιος)
has the same root as the word translated
"righteousness," above (see the discussion of
the righteousness of God, pages 58–63). It indicates living in accordance with law, treating
others equitably, doing the right things.[85]

Live

The word translated "live" is *zaō* (ζάω). In
its various forms, it is one of the most common words used in Romans, especially in the
middle third of the book, which discusses the
Christian life.[86] One could see much, if not all,
of Romans as a treatise on the life of the just,
the life of holiness.

Zaō, "to live," indicates physiological, or
animal, life, as well as life in its fullest sense,
including religious life. The two threads we
have seen before, the spirit and the flesh, continue to be intertwined in the word *live*, for
the life referred to is not a life separated from
the body.

Just as life is life in the concrete flesh as
well as in the spirit, the justice of the faithful
is not abstract. It is incarnate justice, a justice
that is necessarily concrete. Those who are
faithful are satisfied only to be just in real relations with real people. In the Sermon on the
Mount, Christ specifically described what it
means to be faithfully just: in addition to
possessing such personal characteristics as
humility, gentleness, and perseverance in
persecution, the just are compassionate,
peacemaking, respectful of others, forgiving,
and generous both with material things and
in understanding.[87] King Benjamin describes
the just, or the righteous, even more con-
cretely. He says that the just provide for their
children and will not allow them to be at war
with one another, and he speaks at great
length about the fact that they succor those
who are in need (see Mosiah 4:14, 16–23, 26).
The just are those who do the work for others
that needs to be done, work "in the trenches"
on stake and ward welfare projects, in Sunday School and Primary classes, as home and
visiting teachers, in the nursery, by helping
the homeless and poor in the community, and
by teaching disadvantaged adults to read.
The just life of the faithful is a life of unself-
satisfied obligation and service.

It is interesting to note in passing that, as
if to show that there is no higher or lower
duty for the just in the eyes of God, Benjamin

concludes his description of the just life with an admonition to return whatever we borrow (see Mosiah 4:28). In the last half of Mosiah 4, Benjamin moves from the home to the wider community, from peace among children to providing our substance to those who stand in need. It might be tempting to read these verses as a movement from lower to higher things. When compared to what we think of as more important matters, such as retaining a remission of our sins or finding a cure for cancer, returning what we borrow seems insignificant and mundane. But Benjamin pointedly undercuts any attempt on our part to order our obedience as if there were greater and lesser spiritual commandments, as if the body and the spirit were divided against one another with the needs and desires of the spirit taking precedence over those of the body. In the just life, the matters we identify as spiritual and important remain so. But the matters that seem trivial and mundane are as significant as the spiritual matters. In the life of justice, the spirit and the world, or the spirit and the body, are not divided from or against each other.

Faith

The word translated "faith" and its cognates are, with the word *life* and its cognates, perhaps the most important words in the epistle to the Romans. There is much confusion and disagreement about what Paul means when he says that we are saved by grace if we have faith, but there can be little doubt that this is his message. (See the discussion of verse 5, page 31, for more about what faith means in the New Testament and why the alternate translation uses the word *trust*.)

The just shall live by faith

The phrase *the just shall live by faith* is a verse from Habakkuk 2:4, a verse Paul quotes to support his claim that God's righteousness (justice) is revealed from faith to faith. This is why he is not ashamed of the gospel (see Romans 1:16). Habakkuk 2:4 is the scripture on which Paul bases the rest of his letter. Taken with the first part of the verse, this phrase can be best understood as something similar to what Paul says in 2 Corinthians 5:21: "We might be made the righteousness of God in him [Christ]." If we live by faith in Christ, then we will be exemplars of the righteousness, or justice, of God.

One can ask whether the Greek words translated "by faith" modify *the just* or *shall live*.[88] If they modify the former, then the usual translation is correct: "the just shall live through their faith." However, if they modify the latter, then this says "the person who is righteous through faith shall live." There is no way to decide between the two options based on grammar alone. Interpreters make their decision based on the theological assumptions that they bring to Romans. However, the Septuagint version of Habukkuk 2:4 is not ambiguous: "the righteous [or just], through faith in me, shall live." Since this verse seems to be Paul's point of reference, it is reasonable to conclude that *by faith* modifies *the just*: "the just shall live by their faith."

The English translation of this clause may lead us to believe that this is a command, but in Greek it is ambiguous. It can be read as a command, but it can also be read as either a promise or a statement of fact. As in English, these three alternatives cannot always be distinguished grammatically in Greek. Conceptually, promises and statements of fact cannot be distinguished when they are spoken by God. Through their faith, the just will have eternal life. That is a promise of God and thus a fact. On the other hand, some Jewish interpreters have pointed to the verse in Habakkuk as a one-sentence summary of the Mosaic law: those who are righteous live, in other words, remain in the covenant relation to God by their trust in God.[89]

> For therein is the righteousness of God revealed from faith to faith: as it is written, The just shall live by faith.

Given this ambiguity, what are we to make of the quotation from Habakkuk? Is it a promise, a description of the life to come for the exalted, or a command to God's people? As Cranfield points out, the key words of this phrase, *live* and *faith*, can be seen as marking two major subdivisions of Paul's epistle, neither of which can be fully understood without the other.[90] In Romans 1:18–4:25, the first major subdivision of the book, variations on the word *faith* occur thirty-seven times, indicative of the focus on faith in that section. However, in Romans 5:1–8:39, the next major section of the book, the word *faith* occurs only twice, and one of those occurrences is in a summary of Romans 1:18–4:25.

In contrast, in the first subdivision, *life* and its cognates appear only twice, but in the second subdivision they appear twenty-five times. Life is the theme of the second section. We should not overlook this shift in theme when we read Romans, because it marks a development: Paul moves from an understanding of faith to an understanding of the life of faith.

I think Cranfield's observation is important, but I also think he gives insufficient weight to another major section of the book, Romans 9:1–15:13. The movement from faith to the life of faith that we see in Romans 1–8 is the same movement that we see in the letter as a whole: from understanding the necessity of faith and its function to understanding the life that faith requires and makes possible. Romans 9:1–15:13 answers the question of what it means for Israel to be chosen and what the obligations of the saints are, what the life of faith demands.[91] Thus the last part of Romans is the third and last phase of the development that Cranfield has noticed. Paul moves from faith, to the life of faith, to the obligations of faith, or the law. In other words, the chapters of the last major part of Romans are about the other key word in this phrase in verse 17: *just*. (Though my outline [see pages xx–xxi] does not divide the letter this way, one could see Romans 9–11 as parallel to 12–15. Chapters 9–11 deal with God's relation to Israel, while 12–15 deal with his relation to the church.)

It would be fair to say that the central question of Romans is that of the relation of faith to the law, whether the law of Moses or the law written in the hearts of all human beings (see Romans 1:19–20). Paul seems faced with the belief that obedience to the law can bring salvation, that we can put God under obligation by our obedience. He will oppose that belief by arguing that it is not obedience to the law that brings salvation, but faith in Christ. However, at the end of his argument he will reestablish the importance of the law, arguing that obedience is the service we owe to God.

Beginning a sermon with a scriptural quotation, as Paul does in verse 17, is a common method of preaching. A speaker chooses a scripture and uses the sermon to discuss as fully as possible what that scripture means. Sometimes, however, we give the scriptures insufficient respect by talking as if our ideas are most important and the scriptures exist to support our ideas when we need them to do so. Consequently, we sometimes find it difficult to devote more than a minute or two to any particular scripture. We seem to feel that no more than a few minutes' reflection will tell us everything we need to know about that scripture. Obviously, Paul feels otherwise, for he writes an entire book about what one short scripture means.

When some read Habakkuk 2:4 in context, they accuse Paul of "proof-texting." (Proof-texting is using a scripture that appears to back up a particular point of view, whether its context supports that view or not.) Like most, if not all, other ancient writers, Paul does proof-text, but the feeling that proof-texting is wrong is a modern idea, a development of eighteenth-century theories about history and historical documents. This feeling may thus be one of what we call "the philosophies of men" (compare Colossians 2:8). Today we find proof-texting problematic, but, within limits, the ancients did not.

Whether proof-texting is appropriate or inappropriate, the opinion that Paul is proof-texting when he quotes Habakkuk 2:4 may stem from a desire to read his letter as an argument that to be saved by grace alone means that works are unnecessary. However, as we have already seen and as is apparent throughout the letter, Paul is not preaching a separation of faith and works, but explaining the scripture from Habakkuk to clarify the relation of faith to the law. Habakkuk clearly indicates that the just faithfully fulfill the law of Moses; in other words, they faithfully meet the covenantal obligations expressed through that law. Paraphrased, Habakkuk 2:4 could mean "the just (those who do right) live by faith, which has made them just, or obedient." Paul wants us to understand that the righteous are justified by God—made right, brought into the covenant fully—because they are faithfully obedient. Their faith makes them just. The just live by faith now (in their obedience), and because they are faithfully obedient, they will live in the eternities.

In light of what we have learned about the words *just*, *live*, and *faith*, the following paraphrase of Paul's quotation (one of several possible) seems reasonable: "Those who receive life with God live obediently through trusting God." Like Moroni, Paul teaches that right action is made possible only by faith

(see Moroni 7:6–14). Paul shows that faith and obedience to the law are related to each other by pointing out how they are inseparable. James tells us that faith cannot exist without works (see James 2:14–17), and Paul argues that works without faith are also dead, that righteousness comes not in mere obedience to the form of the law, but in obeying in faith. Justice (right judgment, right action, and meeting our obligations to God and others) and faith are not two different things; they are the same thing or two aspects of the same thing.

Paul begins verse 17 by saying that the justice of God—his ability to discriminate between good and evil, to right wrongs, and his faithfulness to his covenants—is revealed in the gospel, the preaching of the life and work and glory of Jesus Christ. After speaking of the Father's justice, Paul describes true justice for mortals: faith and trust in Christ. If we truly exercise our faith in Christ, if we truly trust him, then we will be just, for he has told us we need not worry about ourselves. We will be able to deal with others justly, giving all that we have, with no need to fear how we will fare, for we can rely on his promise of salvation. Just as to do something to one of the least is to do it to Christ, so, too, to be just with others is to trust in Christ, because he guarantees the possibility of ultimate justice. Those who have faith—those who trust God—will, like God, be just. Genuinely just people live by faith. Their trust in God gives their justice a foundation. God is just because he makes our justice possible, and that is something that sometimes seems impossible in a fallen world.

Finally, we might ask why Paul cites a scripture about the justification of the faithful as proof of God's justice (see verse 17). At least two answers seem plausible: (1) there is really only one faithful person: the Son; and

> For therein is the righteousness of God re-
> vealed from faith to faith: as it is written, The
> just shall live by faith.

(2) God's justice is exemplary of the justice of those who are made faithful. That God offers us salvation even though we are not faithful to him (because we sin) proves his infinite justice or righteousness, his ability to right wrongs. To the degree that our sins are removed and we are filled with the Spirit (see Romans 8), we emulate God's justice. As evident in Romans 8:17, that means we will inevitably suffer unjustly.

JST Verse 17

No change.

Verses 18–23

King James

18For the wrath of God is revealed from heaven against all ungodliness and unrighteousness of men, who hold the truth in unrighteousness; 19Because that which may be known of God is manifest in them; for God hath shewed it unto them. 20For the invisible things of him from the creation of the world are clearly seen, being understood by the things that are made, even his eternal power and Godhead; so that they are without excuse: 21Because that, when they knew God, they glorified him not as God, neither were thankful; but became vain in their imaginations, and their foolish heart was darkened. 22Professing themselves to be wise, they became fools, 23And changed the glory of the uncorruptible God into an image made like to corruptible man, and to birds, and fourfooted beasts, and creeping things.

Alternate

18For God's wrath is revealed from heaven against all the impiety and injustice of those who suppress the truth by injustice. 19This occurs because that which is known about God is manifest in them, for God made it manifest in them. 20Since the creation of the world, his unseen attributes, both his eternal power and his divinity, are perceived when they are understood by means of his works. Thus, such persons are without excuse 21because, although they knew God, they did not glorify him as God, nor were they thankful. Instead, they were brought to futility in their speculations, and their undiscerning hearts were darkened. 22Claiming to be wise, they became foolish, 23and they exchanged the glory of the incorruptible God for the likeness of an image of corruptible man, and of birds, and of beasts, and of reptiles.

> For the wrath of God is revealed from heaven against all ungodliness and unrighteousness of men, who hold the truth in unrighteousness;

Verse 18

Having in verse 17 stated his thesis—God's dealings with the faithful reveal his righteousness—Paul begins with the negative formulation of that thesis: the Lord's dealings with the unfaithful. In chapter 1, he discusses the unfaithful among the gentiles. He turns to Israel at the beginning of chapter 2. Romans 1:18–2:11 may be a case of diatribe, a rhetorical form in which one pretends to argue with someone to teach something. If Paul uses diatribe, some of the difficulties we find in reading Romans, such as to whom Paul is referring in Romans 2:1 and what to make of his description of himself in Romans 7:8–23, are solved.

Much of verse 18 and the following verses seems to have been influenced by Wisdom, a book that was popular among the early Christians and often used as scripture. The book is echoed in many places. For example, chapter 1 of Wisdom discusses the necessity of justice, and Wisdom 13:1–10 is much like this section of Romans, explaining how those who worship idols could have known about God (for more on Wisdom, see page 17).

In places, Paul seems to combine Stoic philosophy and Jewish thought, a combination that is also evident in Wisdom. This combination probably does not reflect Paul's education, but contemporary ideas that had also found their way into Wisdom. Because these ideas were current, they likely appealed to the congregation at Rome and were easy to understand because the terms Paul used to describe them were familiar. The Stoics believed a sense of right and wrong is available to every person through reason and contemplation.

Thus, because this part of Stoic philosophy was both familiar to the people of Paul's time and consonant with the gospel, it was useful to Paul as he preached. However, the early leaders of the church clearly rejected other Stoic doctrines, such as their doctrine of fate and the resulting mechanistic attitude toward the creation (see, for example, 2 Peter 3:4–5).

The wrath of God

In verse 17 we saw that divine justice is revealed to those who are faithful. The converse of divine justice is divine wrath, and in the phrase *the wrath of God* we see that divine wrath is revealed to those who are not faithful.

Though the most obvious and literal translation of the Greek word translated "wrath" (*orgē*, ὀργή) is "wrath" or "anger," we must be careful as we think about what this means. On the one hand, we do not want to overlook the fact that anger is attributed to God. On the other hand, we probably do not want to attribute to God the kind of anger we are most familiar with, especially not the blind and blinding anger we associate with the word *wrath*. Notice that we do not see the Father punishing the sinners described later, at least not in our ordinary sense of the word *punish*. Rather, as we will see, Paul says that the Father gives them up to their sins (see verse 24). Their sin is their punishment.

One legitimate understanding of divine wrath is that the Father's wrath is his reaction to evil, his abhorrence of sin. One who judges rightly abhors the evil and sin he condemns, and sinners rightly call that abhorrence wrath. We stand condemned for our sins by the Father's righteous judgment, and from our point of view, *wrath* is a particularly appropriate word. However, *wrath* describes our experience, not God's emotion. On this view, the Father's wrath is his refusal to be indifferent to or permissive with those who sin. In his love for us, he calls us to repentance and demands that we cease to be sinful (see Amos 3:2), often warning us what will happen if we do not. This demand and warning are acts of love, but the sinner experiences them as anger and wrath.

Is revealed

The phrase *is revealed* corresponds to the same phrase in verse 17, making the two verses parallel. In verse 17 the justice of God is revealed in the gospel, and in verse 18 through the end of the chapter the wrath of God is revealed against all sin.

Ungodliness and unrighteousness

Another translation of the phrase *ungodliness and unrighteousness* is "impiety and injustice." In verse 17, God's righteousness, his justice, was revealed. In verses 18–32 (and also in Romans 2:1–11) the injustice, in other words, the unrighteousness, of human beings will be revealed. The mention of ungodliness (*asebeia*, ἀσέβεια, meaning "impiety")[92] prefigures the idolatry of the sinners in verses 21–25. Not to worship God is to worship something else, as is to find something to be more valuable than God. Thus the failure to worship (or to worship properly) can be used as a metonymy for sin in general.

Ungodliness and unrighteousness may be a pleonastic pair (see the discussion of *grace and apostleship* in verse 5, pages 28–30). If so, either the two words are intended to be understood as the same thing or may be translated as "the impiety (or ungodliness) of injustice." To be impious is to transgress one's obligations to God, while to be unjust is to transgress one's obligations to other mortals. God's wrath is revealed on all in each group because they are, in reality, the same. To transgress one is to transgress the other. Paul's mention of both emphasizes the point that God will not con-

done evil, no matter what its form, no matter whom it is against. The Father is no respecter of persons (see Romans 2:11) and will no more accept transgression against another person than he would against himself: "Inasmuch as ye have done it unto one of the least of these my brethren, ye have done it unto me" (Matthew 25:40).

Truth

In New Testament usage, the word translated "truth" (*alētheia*, ἀλήθεια) has basically three meanings: dependability and uprightness (as in Romans 3:7; 15:8); truth in our sense, namely, what corresponds to reality, the opposite of what is false; and finally, reality. The last of these may strike us as odd, but that is at least partly because we think of reality differently than did the people of New Testament times. For us, reality is physical reality. For them it was closer to what we might broadly call moral reality, and this is why the Savior could say, "I am the way, the truth, and the life" (John 14:6).

This supposed failure to separate the moral, or spiritual, realm from the physical is one of the things that most significantly marks the difference between the ancient Greek and Hebrew world and the modern world. Several hundred years before Paul, the Greek philosopher Plato claimed that only the virtuous could have knowledge.[93] Though this idea makes no sense to us (except perhaps metaphorically) because we do not have the same understanding of reality as did the ancients, it is implicit in much Greek and other Mediterranean thought. For example, it is a prominent feature of Stoic philosophy, perhaps the most common philosophy in Paul's day. This identification of virtue with knowledge tells us as much about the ancients' concept of knowledge as it does about their concept of virtue.

> For the wrath of God is revealed from heaven against all ungodliness and unrighteousness of men, who hold the truth in unrighteousness;

For us, what is—reality—is objective rather than personal, and it is ultimately static, "a datum at rest in itself."[94] However, for the ancients, the most real thing is that which makes all other things possible. For Plato, that was the Good. For the Hebrews and Christians, it was God. For the ancients, any discussion of reality that did not take account of what is most real was deficient. Thus they would see our objective descriptions of things as deficient because they explicitly omit reference to the Good or to God.

The implications of this view are numerous. Suffice it to point to just one. Hebrews and early Christians believed that God is ultimately the reality, and for them reality was "pre-eminently *personal being*."[95] All other realities had to be measured against that one. Thus Hebrews and Christians would have agreed with Plato that knowledge is virtue (i.e., being in harmony with the divine), for to know is ultimately to know God, and only the virtuous can know God.[96]

If translated literally, the word translated "truth" (*alētheia*) means "the unhidden." That meaning does not carry over from preclassical Greek times even into classical times, much less into New Testament times, but the etymology is nevertheless sound and informative.[97] With this caveat, we can conclude that Paul and other writers use the Greek word for *truth* in ways similar to the way we use *truth*, but this root meaning can help us understand that truth is revelation. Sin hides or suppresses the truth, and the Lord reveals it again. One of Paul's themes is that the Lord does indeed reveal truth, though he is not obliged to do so. He does it as a gift. For Greek- and Hebrew-speaking people, truth is connected to acquaintance and experience more than to a recitation of facts. This explains why we are free if we know the truth: genuine knowledge is more than the ability to recite a list of facts. Jesus was born on the earth and died to save us, Joseph Smith was a prophet of God, and prophets on the earth today guide us and speak for God. Knowledge is not merely knowing these facts, but living and experiencing them as true. That life and experience, the truth in its ancient sense, frees us.

Though ancient Greek and Hebrew writers would certainly have thought such lists of facts were true, they did not think that a knowledge of those lists was the primary manifestation of truth. Instead, for ancient writers truth was a matter of acquaintance. This follows from their understanding of reality: to know God (or, for the Greeks, what is ultimate) is not to know about him as much as it is to be acquainted with him. Thus while we think a person knows something if he can tell us various facts about it, they would have thought he knew it if he were familiar with it and had experience with it, whether it was a fact, an idea, a thing, or a person.[98] To the ancients, that Heavenly Father knows all things did not mean primarily that he could tell them about everything if he wanted to. It meant instead that he has experienced everything, that he is familiar with all. According to this way of thinking about God's knowledge, God can tell us everything. He is omniscient. This ability to tell us everything is a consequence of his knowledge, but it does not constitute his knowledge.

Knowledge necessarily means knowledge of the truth; it is self-contradictory to know something that is not true. If truth is acquaintance and experience, then genuine knowledge is like that gained by Adam and Eve: a lived, experiential acquaintance with good and evil and God that gives a person the ability to see the difference between good and evil and to choose between them (see Genesis 3; Moses 4). That kind of knowledge is the basis for our ability to be just as our Father in Heaven is just. Such knowledge comes by faith and is absent when we are in sin.

From this point of view, one thinking as did the ancients might go so far as to say that we cannot know evil at all. Evil and what is false are correlates, and we cannot know something false. We can know that something is false, but we cannot know the thing itself—be acquainted with and experience it—unless it is true. I cannot know that the moon is made of green cheese, because it is not. The knowledge of good and evil, then, is an acquaintance or experience with the reality and fullness of what is good (God) and the knowledge that it is possible to deny that fullness (evil). In this sense, Satan has no knowledge because he refuses that experience of God.

Though it sounds strange to our modern ears, given, as we have seen, that one ancient understanding of the word *truth* is "the real," logic implies that evil is unreal. Of course, that is not to say that there is no evil or that it is imaginary or any other thing that we think of when we say that something is unreal. By coming to that conclusion we apply our understanding of reality anachronistically. We use our concept of reality to interpret reality quite differently than did the ancients.

When the ancients said that evil is unreal, they used morality rather than physicality as the measure of reality. When, as ancient thinkers did, we use God as the standard of reality, then we can see a fullness of reality and know that what is ungodly is unreal because it does not measure up to God's standards.

Who hold the truth in unrighteousness

In the phrase *who hold the truth in unrighteousness*, the Greek word *katechō* (κατέχω),

translated "hold," means "to hold captive," hence the alternate translation "to suppress." As before, another translation of the Greek word translated "unrighteousness" is "injustice." People's unrighteousness, their refusal or inability to judge rightly between good and evil and to right wrongs, suppresses the truth. We commonly think of the truth as something that can be believed or at least understood apart from our righteousness. However, as we have seen, for Paul and others of his time, the truth is moral as well as factual. For them, the truth is something one cannot hold without acting on it. To the degree that we are unjust, we suppress the truth and thus cannot know it. Sin and truth are mutually exclusive in the gospel.

We will later see some ways in which people have held the truth captive by their injustices (see pages 83–97).

JST Verse 18

For the wrath of God is revealed from heaven against all ungodliness and unrighteousness of men, <u>who love not the truth, but remain in unrighteousness.</u>

Joseph Smith changes *who hold the truth in righteousness* to *who love not the truth, but remain in unrighteousness*. This shows what it means to hold the truth in unrighteousness. That loving the truth and remaining in unrighteousness are opposed to one another in the JST phrasing suggests that to remain in unrighteousness is not to love the truth. If we do not love the truth, then we will not seek to reveal it. In fact, because our unrighteousness is opposed to the truth, when we are unrighteous we suppress the truth by the very act of being unrighteous. The Prophet's revision clarifies the relation between denying the truth and injustice and states it in contemporary terms, thus making the point more clear for us.

> Because that which may be known of God is manifest in them; for God hath shewed it unto them.

Verse 19

Verse 19 repeats the idea of verse 18 and explains that verse. Verse 18 tells us that God reveals his wrath to the unrighteous, and verse 19 tells us that he does this because he has already shown the unrighteous what they can know of him. Verses 20 and 21 will expand this idea.

Because

Because indicates that the following words explain what accounts for God's wrath.

Known

The Greek word *gnōstos* (γνωστός) has a broad variety of uses. In general, it indicates understanding rather than sensory perception.[99] (That is one reason for thinking that Paul is not presenting a cosmological argument in this and the following verses. See the discussion of verse 20, page 79.) In gnosticism, a movement related to early Christianity and holding some similar doctrines as well as some heretical ones, *gnōstos*, meaning "knowledge," most often refers to what is known by divine illumination. The book of Wisdom (see the discussion on page 17) may use *gnōstos* in a similar manner. "Intimate knowledge" or "intimate acquaintance" is thus a good paraphrase. Given the meaning of *truth* discussed above (verse 18, pages 73–75), this meaning of the word is important, for it bolsters the point that the truth is something one cannot merely hold, but must live. That knowledge is not merely the ability to recite a list of facts, but something intimate, something a person experiences.

That which may be known of God

Literally, the phrase *that which may be known of God* means "the thing known of God." We can read the genitive (the *of*) in two different ways: "the things we know about God" or "the knowledge that comes from God." As we have seen, for Paul, to know about the Father in any full sense is to know not only what his characteristics are (that would be merely to have a list), but also what our relationship to him is and, therefore, what he requires of us. It is to know these things not just as facts, but as elements of our experience. For example, to know that I must not lie is not only to have learned that fact, but to feel that command as an imperative. It is to experience the need not to lie. Such knowledge is from God because it is from our experience of him; it is godly knowledge. Thus the second reading of the genitive, "the knowledge that comes from God," is more appropriate, though it does not exclude our knowing things about God.

In them

The phrase *in them* indicates that not only has God revealed himself to all human beings since the creation of the world, but the fact that he has done so is revealed in those human beings. Even their unrighteousness is a revelation that they know good from evil. We will see below how they have that knowledge in themselves.

Is manifest in them; for God hath shewed it unto them

The King James translation does not take into account a significant wordplay in the Greek version of the phrase *is manifest in them; for God hath shewed it unto them*. The word translated "manifest" (*phaneros*, φανερός) can also be translated "known." It comes from a word meaning "to appear" or "to shine forth." The word translated "hath shewed" (*phaneroō*, φανερόω) is a cognate of *phaneros*. *Phaneroō* could easily be translated "revealed" (though it is not the same verb as that translated "revealed" in verses 17 and 18). Thus one way to translate the phrase would be "is revealed in them, for God has revealed it to them" or "is known to them, for God has made it known to them." Because the word *phaneros* carries with it the idea of shining forth—of light—another translation is possible: "is clear to them for God made it clear to them." But since the Greek also carries with it the notion that the manifestation is in them already and not merely an observation or the result of an observation, the alternate translation is "is manifest in them, for God made it manifest in them."

One might suppose that most people act unjustly because they are ignorant. However, if they are truly ignorant, then they are not accountable for their sins, and God will not punish them for those sins (though he might allow them to suffer for other reasons, since, as Christ's life demonstrates, even the just suffer). Paul does not believe that for the most part we act unjustly out of ignorance; he says that all people, including those who are impious and unjust, have already had piety and justice revealed to them.

For modern people this is a strange notion. How is it possible, we might ask, for everyone to already know piety and justice? For people of Paul's time the answer was not particularly difficult. Though many disagreed about the details, most thought of truth as something like harmony[100] (recall the earlier discussion of *truth*, verse 18, pages 73–75). Knowing the truth meant being in harmony with the way things really are. Ancient people tended to think of truth as a way of being, or fitting into the reality of the world, and that is why ancient Greek thinkers thought it obvious that only virtuous people could know the truth. Virtue meant acting in harmony with reality.

For those who, like the Greeks and the Hebrews and other ancients, think that truth is a matter of harmony, everyone who lives at all is in harmony with the world to some extent or another. People must be able to get along in the real world to some degree. They must be in harmony with it enough to eat and drink and to avoid falling into pits in broad daylight. If they were not, they could not survive. Gaining knowledge, or virtue, is a matter of becoming more and more in harmony with what is most real, the source for or model of the world we live in. It is a matter of getting rid of things that create disharmony. Because, from this ancient point of view, everyone must be in harmony with the world to some degree, everyone already knows what the truth is, or they at least know it sufficiently to learn more. No one starts from zero, so no one is incapable of being virtuous.

Given this understanding of truth and our relation to it, Paul can appeal to the creation of the world as the standard of truth: God created a harmonious world, people live in that world and are necessarily in harmony with it to some degree, and every person can thus become more harmonious and act rightly by developing the harmony in which they already live. Those who do not do this go against the testimony of their own lives, a testimony that God has provided to everyone.

Though this is not the way we usually think of the light of Christ today (we think of it as a power or an ability rather than a function of our own existence), this is generally the way most people of Paul's time would have thought of our ability to know right from wrong,[101] and it is probably what lies behind Paul's remarks in verses 19 and 20. Paul is speaking of the light of Christ, though not in ways that are familiar to us.

> For the invisible things of him from the creation of the world are clearly seen, being understood by the things that are made, even his eternal power and Godhead; so that they are without excuse:

JST Verse 19

<u>After</u> that which may be known of God is manifest <u>to</u> them //.

The changes in the JST are slight, but significant. Joseph Smith joins this verse to the previous one with the word *after* rather than *because*, he changes *in* to *to*, and he deletes the phrase *for God hath shewed it unto them* that appears in the KJV at the end of the verse.

To understand the first of these changes, we must see the change in the context of verses 18 and 19 together. The King James translation of verses 18 and 19 can be paraphrased in this way: "God's wrath is revealed against all the unrighteousness of people who remain in unrighteousness, and it is revealed against them because what can be known of God is revealed in them." Verses 18 and 19 of the JST read, "God's wrath is revealed against all the unrighteousness of people who remain in unrighteousness and do not love the truth, even after what can be known of God is revealed to them."

As we have seen with several other changes the Prophet made, the difference is not so much a change in meaning as it is a change in emphasis. The Greek and King James texts use verse 19 as an explanation of why God's wrath can be revealed to the unrighteous. Joseph Smith's text ignores that question and uses verse 19 to emphasize the unrighteousness of those who love evil and not truth. The King James and Greek understandings of these verses emphasize divine wrath and how people suppress the truth. The Joseph Smith translation emphasizes the sinfulness of those who suppress the truth, balancing that, as it were, with divine wrath.

By changing *in* to *to*, Joseph Smith changes the meaning. The traditional text says that the unrighteous know of God because that knowledge is revealed in the people themselves, and it is revealed in them because God made them and the world. The Prophet's change deletes the idea that the knowledge of God is shown in the unrighteous.

Verse 20

The invisible things

The translation "the invisible things" is excellent because the English word carries many of the same connotations as does the Greek. Paul contrasts what can be seen with what cannot. The Greek word he used in verse 19, when he spoke of "that which may be known of God," implies that the things of God cannot be seen by the eye. In verse 20 he refers to those things once again, calling them invisible, or not visible to the eye.

Of him

As is often the case, the question is how to read the *of* in *of him*. Given the earlier discussion of the things of God (see the commentary on verse 19), it is reasonable to read this as "from him."

The world

The word translated "world" (*kosmos*, κόσμος) refers not simply to the planet earth, but to the created universe. "Cosmos," a transliteration of the Greek word, is a good translation.

From the creation of the world

The Greek word translated "from" (*apo*, ἀπό) in the phrase *from the creation of the world* could also be translated "since," in other words, "since the creation of the world." Sometimes this Greek word is used to indicate the originating point of a particular thing.[102] The most obvious meaning in this context is "since." Nevertheless, I think the other meaning carries an important connotation: the knowledge Paul is speaking of had its beginning in the creation, and the creation itself, of which we are part, gives us the knowledge of God.

The invisible things of him from the creation of the world are clearly seen

The phrase *the invisible things of him from the creation of the world are clearly seen* is Paul's explanation of why he rejects the assumption that people act unjustly out of ignorance: since the beginning of the world and implicit in its creation, invisible things like the truth are clearly known to those who choose to understand them through God's works. Isaiah has said the same thing (see Isaiah 40:21–23), and so has Alma (see Alma 30:41–44). No one is incapable of knowing the truth if they will honestly strive to do so, if they will honestly give up ignoring it. We are capable of this because the Father has already given the truth to us, and he has made us so that we are in harmony with it unless we give up that harmony. Presumably, one way to explain the need for an atonement is that, being fallen, we are out of harmony with God. We have refused to be in harmony with him. However, even if we cease to refuse this harmony, something more than our own effort is needed to restore it.

Being understood by the things that are made

If we contemplate the visible things that the Father has made, such as the natural world, then we can understand what is supposedly not visible to us, namely, God's power and his divinity. At first glance it might seem that Paul is offering proof of God's existence with the phrase *being understood by the things that are made*, proof based on the order of the universe (what philosophers call cosmological proof), but I do not think he is. Paul is explaining that each person can discriminate between good and evil, and this has been true from the beginning of the world. That is the way we and the world were created. Though we may not know what to call our knowledge of good and evil or how to explain that knowledge, if we understand the world and our existence in it (which we necessarily do; see the discussion of *truth* in verse 18, pages 73–75, and the discussion of *is manifest in them; for God shewed it unto them* in verse 19, pages 76–77), we know what we need to know. Our human existence in the world with other humans shows us the basics of right and wrong.

As shown by the endowment ceremony and the various versions of the story of Adam and Eve in the garden, the ability to discriminate between good and evil is central to the plan of salvation and our understanding of our place in the world. If we are evil it is because we refuse to be good, not because we cannot be good or even because we are ignorant. Though we may be ignorant of the finer points of what we should do, if we are genuinely serious and aware of the world and the way we live in it, we are able to see what is right and what is wrong. Both we and the world are made in such a way that seeing that difference is always possible unless we refuse to allow it to be. Every person has the light of Christ (see D&C 84:45–46). Therefore, Paul says, those who are impious and unjust have no excuse.

Eternal power

One of the things we see if we look at the world attentively is the power of God. The

> Because that, when they knew God, they glori-
> fied him not as God, neither were thankful;
> but became vain in their imaginations, and
> their foolish heart was darkened.

word *power* translates the Greek word *dynamis* (δύναμις), from which we get words like *dynamic*. The emphasis of the Greek word *power* in the phrase *his eternal power* is not on sheer strength or power to overcome, as seems to be the case with the English word *power,* but on the ability to act.[103] The world reveals God's ability to act. It shows his eternal ability to create, and more. If the Father has eternal power, or infinite ability to act—in other words, if his power to act does not come to an end—then he has power to save us. The creation of the world guarantees God's ability to do what needs to be done for us. Nothing can stop him from acting.

Godhead

"Divinity" is a more accurate translation of *theotes* (θεότης), translated "Godhead," though perhaps *divinity* and *Godhead* can be synonyms. In the creation, we see the divinity of God, the things that make him God. What are those things? One mentioned in the phrase within which the word *Godhead* appears is his creative power, something that distinguishes him from the supposed divinity of the false gods, idols that are made and cannot make anything themselves. As we learn in the temple, creative power, the power to be a parent, is the mark of true divinity. Another of the distinguishing characteristics of the Divine is righteousness, or justice. Given the earlier discussion of God's righteousness (see the discussion of *the righteousness of God* in verse 17, pages 58–63), and the contrast that Paul makes between divine righteousness and human unrighteousness, it seems reasonable to assume that Paul is suggesting that we can see divine righteousness in the creation. If so, we presumably see it in the Father's making the world harmoniously and thereby making it possible for us to have harmony in our lives (compare the discussion of *is manifest in them; for God hath shewed it unto them* in verse 19, pages 76–77).

His eternal power and Godhead

As a whole, the phrase *his eternal power and Godhead* describes the unseen things that an attentive understanding of the world allows us to see. God has created the world so that, by being part of the world, we have what Latter-day revelation calls the light of Christ (see Alma 28:14; Moroni 7:19; D&C 84:45–46), and it allows us to see the difference between good and evil. But to know the good is to know God, even if only implicitly, for whatever persuades us to do good is of God (see Moroni 7:16). Thus, if we have the light of Christ then we know the power of God. We experience it even if we do not have cognitive understanding of it. Implicit in our experience of life in the world is the knowledge that God has the power to do good and to persuade us to do good. With this knowledge, which is not necessarily explicit or cognitive, we also know what it is that makes him God; we know what the verse calls his Godhead. We also know that these godly attributes are what make him the ruler of the world with infinite creative power. To know he is the omnipotent ruler is to know we need not fear that Satan will win the confrontation between good and evil, for our Father has the eternal power to bring about good. Notice the difference between having the power to defeat evil and having the power always to do good. These verses suggest that the Father's divinity is found in the latter rather than the former. Thus the light of Christ is the basis for our faith in God, our trust in him. We can refuse to trust if we wish, but we have already been given sufficient knowledge for us to have faith if we do not refuse. This is one way in which even our faith in God is a gift from him to us.

The phrase *his eternal power and Godhead* also may be a pleonastic pair, which is a pair of phrases intended to have the same meaning, but used together for emphasis (see the discussion of verse 5, pages 29–30, for more about pleonastic pairs). If it is such a pair, the phrase defines God's divinity as his eternal ability to act.

Without excuse

The Greek word *apologia* (ἀπολογία), translated "excuse" in the phrase *without excuse*, can also be translated "explanation." There is no explanation for sin. That strikes modern ears as strange, for our scientific way of thinking tells us that everything can be explained. However, if why people are evil could be explained, we would excuse it. To truly explain sin is to describe what causes it, and if it is caused, then those who commit sin are not responsible for doing so. In the sense of naming a cause, there is no explanation for sin except for the sinners themselves.

JST Verse 20

For <u>God hath revealed unto them</u> the invisible things of him, from the creation of the world<u>, which</u> are clearly seen<u>; things which are not seen</u> being understood by the things that are made, <u>through</u> his eternal power and Godhead; so that they are without excuse;

The traditional version of this verse and Joseph Smith's revised version of it explain how the unrighteous have had a revelation of God. The Prophet's version makes this more apparent with the insertion of *God hath revealed unto them*, a repetition of the underlying theme of this section of Paul's letter. In the traditional text, this clause is passive, but Joseph Smith makes it active and therefore more readable. In addition, he changes *clearly seen* from a phrase telling us how the things of God are revealed to a phrase describing the things God has revealed. The third change, the addition of *things which are not seen*, ties the two clauses together, making it clear that Paul is still speaking of the invisible things of God, including the ability of created beings to understand what they cannot see. The final change identifies divine eternal power and Godhead not as things that created beings see, in other words, the creations of God, but as the method by which they see them.

Verse 21

When they knew God, they glorified him not as God

The Greek version of the phrase *when they knew God, they glorified him not as God* is even more powerful than the English. Literally and therefore awkwardly it reads, "having known God, not as God they glorified him nor were thankful," and can mean "though they knew God, they did not give the glory due to him as God and they were not thankful to him."

When they knew God

Those against whom God has directed his wrath may not have known him personally, but they have known him through the light of Christ, in other words, through knowing what it means to be a person created by God in a world created by him. The word translated "knew" in the phrase *when they knew God* is the same word used in verse 19 (*gnōstos*, γνωστός) and connotes an intimate knowledge. Recipients of God's wrath know not just facts about him and his creation and hence good and evil, but are intimately acquainted with these things through their experience.

> Professing themselves to be wise, they became fools, And changed the glory of the uncorruptible God into an image made like to corruptible man, and to birds, and fourfooted beasts, and creeping things.

They glorified him not as God

Had sinners acknowledged what they knew through the light of Christ and acted rightly, they would have glorified God. But because they have sinned, they cannot glorify God as he is. Sin is implicitly but necessarily a denial of the Father. A refusal of his righteousness and justice is equally a refusal of him, because that righteousness and justice are an essential part of what he is. Therefore, even if those enmeshed in sin seem to glorify the Father, they necessarily glorify something else, and to glorify something other than the Father is idolatry. Idolatry is at the heart of an absent conscience, for both are the refusal to recognize God as God.

Neither were they thankful

The word translated "were thankful" (*eucharisteō*, ἐυχαριστέω) in the phrase *neither were they thankful* has as one of its roots the word for *grace*, or *charis* (χάρις). They refused to accept God's grace—in this case, the light of Christ—so they were not thankful. They have the gift, but they refuse to recognize that they have it; they are ingrates. Doctrine and Covenants 59:21 notes the following about ingratitude: "And in nothing doth man offend God, or against none is his wrath kindled, save those who confess not his hand in all things, and obey not his commandments."

But became vain in their imaginations

In contemporary English, "imaginations" is not as good a translation as "thoughts," "reasonings," or "speculations" would be in the phrase *but became vain in their imaginations* (the Greek word is *dialogismos*, διαλογισμός).

When they thought about God, they did so futilely, fruitlessly, profitlessly. Their sinfulness and their refusal to see God's power and Godhead in the world made their thinking profitless.

Vain

The Greek word translated "vain" (*mataioō*, ματαιόω) meaning "useless" or "futile," translates the Hebrew word that denotes idols, "vain things" (*hebel*, הֶבֶל; see Acts 14:15 for the Greek and Leviticus 17:7; Jeremiah 2:5; and 2 Kings 17:15 for the corresponding Hebrew). Their reasonings were not only useless, but also idolatrous, as we will see in verse 23. This repeats the idea that "they glorified him not as God."

Imaginations

As mentioned above, another translation of *dialogismos*, is "speculations" or "reasonings," rather than "imaginations." *Dialogismos* is often, if not always, used negatively in the New Testament[104] and refers to the undisciplined use of the mind, especially in service to a corrupt heart, as here. This is why the King James translators used the word *imaginations*.

Heart

The people of Paul's time considered the heart to be the seat of the human being.[105] The heart can connote such things as counsel and courage, as well as wisdom and feeling.

Foolish heart

The Greek word translated "foolish" (*asunetos*, ἀσύνετος) could also be translated "intelligent," "sagacious," "wise," "discerning," or "having good sense" without its negative prefix (like *un-* in English). Sinners have a heart that, as Paul has just shown, lacks wisdom. Their heart does not understand the creation and refuses to discern between good and evil.

Their foolish heart was darkened

By refusing to discern good from evil, they darkened the light that would make it possible for them to discern.

JST Verse 21

Because that, when they knew God, they glorified him not as God, neither were they thankful, but became vain in their imaginations, and their foolish <u>hearts were</u> darkened.

The first change is minor: a semicolon becomes a comma. This may simply reflect the fact that nineteenth-century punctuation conventions were different than those of the sixteenth and seventeenth centuries, when the King James translation was made. The second change is more significant. The Prophet makes the abstract noun *heart* more concrete by changing it to a plural noun. By using the abstract noun, the Greek and the King James Version emphasize the idolaters as a group. The Prophet's change shifts that emphasis to the individuals.

Verses 22–23

Verses 22 and 23 may be read as an explanation of the foolishness of the people described in verses 23–32. These people claim to be wise but have been made foolish. They are sinful because they have claimed to be wise. They vaunt themselves and in so doing refuse to see what God has placed before their eyes in the creation of the world. The result is their sin, their foolishness.

Verse 22

Professing themselves to be wise, they became fools

The phrase *professing themselves to be wise, they became fools* tells us that, while claiming to be wise, idolaters were actually stupefied by their sinfulness. In Greek, the root word translated "became fools" (*mōrainō*, μωραίνω) means "stupid, silly, or foolish." It is the root for our word *moron*. The verb is passive. This is what happens to those who claim to be wise, especially when the wisdom they profess denies what God has made manifest in them and all around them.

JST Verse 22

No change.

Verse 23

Changed the glory of the uncorruptible God into an image

(See Psalm 106:20; Isaiah 40:19–20; 44:9–20; 45:16.) The sinners Paul describes in the phrase *changed the glory of the uncorruptible God into an image* exchanged the truth of God, which God had implanted in their hearts by creating them, for the lie of idolatry. They worshiped the creature more than the Creator. The irony is that the very creation they worshiped would have revealed the truth of God to them—a truth about his glory that would have glorified them—if they had been willing to understand it (see verse 20). Not to be holy as the Lord God is holy (see Leviticus 19:2) is to be an idolater. Paul is almost certainly specifically thinking of those whose culture is fundamentally Greek, which would include most Romans, but he is using them as a type for all sinners.

Uncorruptible . . . corruptible

The Greek words translated as "uncorruptible" and "corruptible" mean "immortal" and "mortal," respectively (*aphthartos*, ἄφθαρτος; *phthartos*, φθαρτός). The idea is that mortal bodies are corruptible (they are subject to disease, decay, and so on) and thus perish. Immortal bodies, on the other hand, are not subject to such corruption and do not perish. By extension, this contrast may also refer to the major difference between humans and

And changed the glory of the uncorruptible God into an image made like to corruptible man, and to birds, and fourfooted beasts, and creeping things.

God: sin. God is not corruptible, but humans are subject to moral decay.

JST Verse 23

No change.

Verses 24–32

<table>
<tr><td>

King James

₂₄Wherefore God also gave them up to uncleanness through the lusts of their own hearts, to dishonour their own bodies between themselves: ₂₅Who changed the truth of God into a lie, and worshipped and served the creature more than the Creator, who is blessed for ever. Amen. ₂₆For this cause God gave them up unto vile affections: for even their women did change the natural use into that which is against nature: ₂₇And likewise also the men, leaving the natural use of the woman, burned in their lust toward one another; men with men working that which is unseemly, and receiving in themselves that recompence of their error which was meet. ₂₈And even as they did not like to retain God in their knowledge, God gave them over to a reprobate mind, to do those things which are not convenient; ₂₉Being filled with all unrighteousness, fornication, wickedness, covetousness, maliciousness; full of envy, murder, debate, deceit, malignity; whisperers, ₃₀Backbiters, haters of God, despiteful, proud, boasters, inventors of

</td><td>

Alternate

₂₄For this reason, God abandoned them in the lusts of their hearts to uncleanness that they might dishonor their bodies with one another; ₂₅they exchanged the truth of God for the lie and worshipped and served the created thing in place of the Creator, who is to be praised for eternity. Amen. ₂₆This is why God gave them over to dishonorable passions: even their females changed the natural use to that against nature. ₂₇In the same way, the males, having forsaken the natural use of the female, burned up in their lust toward one another, males acting out shamefulness among males, and receiving in return the reward that was appropriate to their self-deceit. ₂₈Just as they did not think it fit to maintain a knowledge of God, God left them to an unfit mind, to do the things that are improper: ₂₉having been filled with all injustice, malice, insatiability, and vice; full of envy, murder, quarrels, deceit, and conspiracy; being gossips, ₃₀slanderers, God-haters, over-reaching, proud, braggarts, devisers of evil, disobedient

</td></tr>
</table>

King James

evil things, disobedient to parents, ₃₁Without understanding, covenantbreakers, without natural affection, implacable, unmerciful: ₃₂Who knowing the judgment of God, that they which commit such things are worthy of death, not only do the same, but have pleasure in them that do them.

Alternate

to parents, ₃₁undiscerning, covenant breaking, unloving, and unmerciful—₃₂they are they who, having known the judgment of God, namely, that those who practice such things are worthy of death, not only do them, but also approve of those who practice them.

Verse 24

Wherefore

In Greek, *wherefore* (*dio*, διό) is a strong connective. Paul uses it to refer to verses 22 and 23, and this connection can help us understand verse 24 to mean "because people are such fools, God gave them up to sin."

Gave them up

"Gave them up" is a literal translation of the verb *paradidōmi* (παραδίδωμι), but "abandon," in the alternate translation, more fully captures the awfulness of what is described. Idolaters abandon God and are, in turn and perhaps necessarily, abandoned by him until they repent. This is the same word translated "gave them up" and "gave them over" in verses 26 and 28.

Uncleanness

The Greek word *akatharsia* (ἀκαθαρσία), translated "uncleanness," means "what is impure," "refuse," or "filth." We could understand this to mean "unatonement," though that would probably not be a good translation of the Greek word. The Father is clean and pure. When idolaters refuse to be clean, they refuse to be at one with him. God punishes them by allowing them to be alienated from him. The book of Wisdom says much the same thing in its assertion that the instru-

ments of sin are the instruments of punishment (see Wisdom 11:16 and page 17 for more on the book of Wisdom). Just as virtue is its own reward, sin is its own punishment. As Alma says, "Wickedness never was happiness" (Alma 41:10). Those who sin have chosen not to live in harmony with the world God has created. That harmony is a unity with the will of the Father and, therefore, with the rest of creation. The Father allows those who sin to live in the disharmony they have created, outside the unity that is possible and thus outside the at-one-ment that is possible. Sinners thereby deny the atonement of Christ, which makes possible our return to at-one-ment with the will of God.

God also gave them up to uncleanness

Failure to worship God is sin, and sin is a consequence of that failure to worship. This is evident in the phrase *God also gave them up to uncleanness*. Failing to recognize God as God results in the sin of idolatry. God not only permits idolaters to sin, he gives them over to their sins and to the lust and dishonor they feel is their just reward. He gives idolaters what they say they want. If we envy the sins of others, then we are not yet converted. If we were converted, we would realize that they cannot be happy in their sins and would not see their experience as either happy or even pleasurable in any fundamental way. Verse 24 explains why this is so: when we sin, we are given up to our sins and lose God. To lose God is to lose everything, just as to gain him is to gain everything (compare D&C 84:38). When the creature loses its connection to the Creator, it loses the meaning of its existence. As the ancients would say, it becomes unreal.

To dishonour

To dishonour (atimazō, ἀτιμάζω) means "to treat shamefully." In verse 26, the same word is translated "vile affections."

To dishonour their own bodies between themselves

As we see in the phrase *to dishonour their own bodies between themselves*, when we commit idolatry—in the broadest sense, all sin—we disgrace our own bodies. We do what we are ashamed of. Spiritual death results in physical shame, in the self-disgrace of the body. This implies that in the absence of sin we would not be ashamed of our bodies; we would not disgrace them.

JST Verse 24

No change.

Verse 25

This verse continues the sentence begun in verse 24. Verses 24 and 25 together form an inclusion. Inclusion is a rhetorical device that is similar to chiasmus but not as structured. The material is "sandwiched" between an idea or phrase that appears both before and after it.

> Wherefore [in other words, because men foolishly worship something other than God (verse 24, referring to verses 21 and 22)],
> > God gave them up to the uncleanness of their hearts [verse 24]—
> namely, those who worshipped the creature more than the Creator [verse 25, referring to verses 22 and 23].

Who

The antecedent of *who* is *them*—the wicked—in verse 24.

Into

As the alternate translation shows, "into" is not as accurate a translation of *en* (ἐν) as "for." This verse uses the language of exchange: those who abandon God for idol worship exchange one thing for another. In chapter three, Paul capitalizes on this idea, using the language of economics and business to discuss our relation to God.

Lie

Lie is the Greek *pseudei* (Ψεύδει) and means not just a lie, but what is false or unreal.

Who changed the truth of God into a lie

From the phrase *who changed the truth of God into a lie*, we can see that the truth of God is that through faith in Jesus Christ we can again be a part of the Father's orderly, harmonious creation (see the discussion of *truth* in verse 18, pages 73–75). Those who, by sinning, refuse to recognize God exchange this truth for the lie that the world is ordered by someone or something other than God. Sometimes when we sin we think that our own desires order the world. Other times we think it is ordered only by supposedly natural processes, and still other times we let the world and our lives be ordered by greed and self-interest. In all cases, sinners give up the truth of God for idolatry.

Worshipped

The verb translated "worshipped" (sebazomai, σεβάζομαι) has the same root as does the word for *impiety* in verse 18 (asebeia).

> For this cause God gave them up unto vile affections: for even their women did change the natural use into that which is against nature: And likewise also the men, leaving the natural use of the woman, burned in their lust toward one another; men with men working that which is unseemly, and receiving in themselves that recompence of their error which was meet.

Served

The verb translated "served" (*latreuō*, λατρεύω) is the same verb used in verse 9, where Paul served God with his spirit. Here we see that because idolaters refuse to recognize God with their spirits, with their bodies they serve the world that God created. Idolatry is refusing to serve God.

And worshipped and served the creature more than the Creator

In the phrase *and worshipped and served the creature more than the Creator*, Paul continues to use the language of exchange. Idolaters worship what is created rather than the Creator. As the alternate translation suggests, they worship the created world "in place of" its Creator. They may worship the world itself, things in that world, idols, or other humans. They probably worship themselves in addition to whatever else they claim to worship. In any case, they worship the creation—the creature—rather than the Creator.

Sin is always idolatrous because it replaces God, who should be in our hearts, with something else. This is why sin is adulterous and why adultery is idolatrous (see below, page 89). Sin replaces the Creator with one of his creations. When our eye is on something other than the Father, we value something more than we value him. Thus, when our eye is not single to his glory (see, for example, D&C 4), or when we sin, we are idolaters.

The Creator, who is blessed for ever

The Greek word translated "is blessed" (*eulogētos*, εὐλογητός) in the phrase *the Creator, who is blessed for ever* is passive and means "to be praised." It refers only to God in the New Testament.[106] The Creator is the one whom we are to praise. Unlike the idols of the sinful, the Father is praised for eternity, and the righteous bless him for eternity because he has given us the gospel through his Son, Jesus Christ. In spite of the fact that the sinful make a lie of his truth (in the words of verse 18, they hold it captive), God will be praised forever. Their lie cannot prevail, presumably because he continues to have the power to do good.

Amen

We use *amen* to mean something like "so be it." Our word is a transliteration of a Hebrew word (*ʾamez*, אָמֵז) that means, approximately, "certain, sure or firm."[107] Incidentally, the King James New Testament consistently translates *amen* as "verily." In Hebrew, *amen* indicates resolve, and this is why it is an appropriate ending to prayers. Paul uses it in the sense of certainty: it is certain that God will be praised forever.

JST Verse 25

No change.

Verses 26–27

Just as verse 25 referred to verse 23, verse 26 repeats verse 24 and adds an example of how some disgrace their bodies: people have turned to homosexual practices.

Burned in their lust

The phrase *burned in their lust* indicates that some have succumbed to homosexual practices. Paul presents this behavior as a type for sexual sin in general. In the Old Testament, idolatry is almost always associated with sexual sin, in part because idolatry often involved sexual sin, though it also stems from the connection between sin and idolatry noted in the discussion of verse 25. In fact, the connection between sexual sin and idolatry was so strong that *adultery* and *idolatry* could be used as synonyms. (The similarity of sound of the two English words makes the connection even more apparent for us.) For example, the book of Hosea is entirely devoted to the use of this association of sexual sin and idolatry. In a call to Israel to repent, the book focuses on Israel's relation to God and portrays it as one of marriage. Paul does not think it a coincidence that the idol-worshiping people of the Greco-Roman world allow homosexual practices. He contrasts the creative power of God with the noncreative sin of homosexual practice.

Sexual sin is particularly obvious as a kind of idolatry. It makes sexuality into a lie; it makes it false and then worships that falseness. It mocks God profoundly, for it changes his glory—eternal increase, the creative power that marks his Godhead—into something profane. For many, lust for the flesh, either heterosexual or homosexual, replaces godly desire.

Of course, godly desire does not negate our existence in the flesh, and the opposite of lust is not celibacy. Sexuality is very much part of what our Father has made us and, therefore, a part of what he wants us to be. Genuine, virtuous, godly sexuality is far more than mere self-gratifying lust. Ironically, lust confuses need with desire, substituting the satiable want of something (lust) for the insatiable attraction to someone (desire).[108] If I am hungry, I have the need to eat. That need orients me to apples, oranges, and other food that will satisfy my need, things used up in satisfying my need, which will, at least temporarily, cease when it is satisfied. The desire

I have for my wife is not like the need I have for an apple. My desire for her is increased by our relation to one another and cannot be satiated. In other words, our relation is not one in which either of us is used up. My love for her is gratifying in a different way than satisfying a need is gratifying.

It seems to follow that if my relation to another person is confused, a matter of lust rather than desire, it cannot be a gratifying relation. Lust expects satiety and another person cannot provide that. Thus, because lust does not really gratify, though it tries to, virtuous sexuality is more pleasurable than unvirtuous sexuality. Like all sin, lust cannot attain the thing it supposedly seeks after so diligently, while virtue, in doing what is right unselfishly and seeking the glory of God, receives what lust seeks and more.

Working

The Greek word *katergazdomai* (κατεργά-ζομαι), translated "working," is one of Paul's favorite words, especially when he talks about sinning.[109] It means "to achieve," "to accomplish," or "to bring about, produce, [or] create" something.[110] Paul's use of this word may run counter to our expectations because he consistently connects work and accomplishment with sin rather than with more positive things. This unusual use follows from his understanding of our relation to God. When we refuse the slavery to God that we are obligated to fulfill, our so-called accomplishments amount to nothing more than sin. On the other hand, when we recognize our slavery to God, we achieve nothing of ourselves. We do nothing, because everything that is done is the will of God. It is his work, not ours. Christians acknowledge that they can do nothing but what God does through them. The sinful wrongly believe that they can accomplish something by their own power.

> And even as they did not like to retain God in their knowledge, God gave them over to a reprobate mind, to do those things which are not convenient;

This understanding of accomplishment does not necessarily imply quietism, waiting for God to do something. We are required to be "anxiously engaged in a good cause, and do many things of [our] own free will" (D&C 58:27) without assuming that what we do is our own. Similarly, a wise steward can make a profit on his master's money, but the money remains the master's and the accomplishment is also the master's (see Matthew 25:13–20; Luke 17:7–10).[111]

That which is unseemly

The Greek word *aschēmosunē* (ἀσχημοσύνη) means "what is shameful" or "what cannot be presented in public." Here it is translated "that which is unseemly." In the Septuagint it refers to the genitalia as well as to excrement (see Exodus 20:26; Leviticus 18:6–19; Deuteronomy 23:14).

Receiving

The word *apolambanō* (ἀπολαμβάνω), translated "receiving," implies not just receiving, but receiving a reward.[112] The Greeks Paul speaks of have accomplished indecency, and in return they receive the reward appropriate to what they have accomplished: they are allowed to be what they have made themselves (see verses 26 and 28). Sin is their reward.

King Benjamin teaches that we must acknowledge our own nothingness (see Mosiah 4:5–11). He also teaches that doing so will bring joy in this life as well as a remission of sins, in other words, both temporal and spiritual salvation (see Mosiah 4:12–29). Only

when we know that we are nothing can we be saved. Thinking he is nothing, the repentant person receives everything. In contrast, the sinner, thinking that he has accomplished something, discovers his own nothingness in the nothingness of his sin. Thinking he is something, he receives nothing.

In themselves

As evidenced by the phrase *in themselves*, idolaters receive their sins into themselves. Those sins become part of what they are, and the idolaters are defined by their sins, or their nothingness, rather than by God's blessings and righteousness.

Recompence

The Greek word *antimisthia* (ἀντιμισθία), translated "recompence," is a word for *reward* that emphasizes the "reciprocal nature of the transaction."[113] Paul continues to use the language of exchange, introducing the question of grace versus works: do we earn salvation in exchange for what we do for God? In Romans 4:2–16 Paul will argue that the answer is no. He can call himself and, implicitly, all believers slaves of God because we must act, but we do not earn. Paul uses the word *recompence* to show that the only thing that we can earn is the reward appropriate for our sinful lives. As we will see in verse 32, that reward is death.

Their error

Literally, *their error* means "their deceit" or "their deceit of themselves" (*planē aōtōn*, πλάνη αὠτῶν). The word *error* is not incorrect, and neither is something like *straying*, as found in some translations, but *error* is not as strong as the Greek word *planē*. The alternate translation translates *their error* as "self-deceit" to capture this stronger meaning. The sins of these people are a deceit, as the previous verses have fully explained. Their sin is not only a mistake, it is an act of self-deceit. Sinners go against what they know to be true by the light of Christ, their own existence.

Meet

Meet means "appropriate."

JST Verses 26–27

No change.

Verse 28

To retain God in their knowledge

The Greek word translated "knowledge" (*epignōsis*, ἐπίγνωσις) is emphatic, meaning something like "full knowledge." The prefix, *epi*, gives it emphasis. The word can also mean "recognition" or even "decision" or "conscience." It is related to the word for *known* in verse 19. The word indicates activity, something people do rather than something that happens to them. This phrase could also be translated "they did not think it fit to recognize God." These people were not merely unknowing, they refused to know God. As the discussion of verse 27 points out, they have deceived themselves. Another way to look at this is that those whom Paul describes have refused to recognize their ability to judge good from evil and the knowledge they have gained in their experience of the world. In other words, they have refused the light of Christ. As a result, they have refused to experience God; they have refused to know him.

God gave them over

In the phrase *God gave them over*, Paul repeats what he said in verse 24. The question might arise why he speaks of their sins as something God has done even indirectly. The alternate translation "left them to" helps clarify that Paul does not mean that God played any

role in their sins. However, at least partly as a reaction to the idolatry to which Israel was always succumbing, the Old Testament prophets rarely ascribe anything in their writings to a power other than God. For example, we read that "he [the Lord] hardened Pharaoh's heart" (Exodus 7:13). As Joseph Smith's revision, "Pharaoh hardened his heart," makes clear, this does not mean that the Lord took the Pharaoh's agency from him and forced him to have a hard heart. Ascribing events such as this to God's power was a literary convention of the Old Testament writers.[114] They knew that the Lord had not forced Pharaoh to have a hard heart, but to show the subservience of every power—including the Pharaoh—to God, they ascribed all significant actions to the Lord. Perhaps they also did this to help prevent idolaters from using the scriptures to show the power of their idols. Pharaoh was worshiped and was thus an idol. The prophets seem to have thought that even though the Lord allows people to choose for themselves, it was appropriate to ascribe what happened to the Lord. They wanted people who read this story to understand that the Lord is always in control, although Pharaoh obviously could choose whether to harden his heart.

The scriptures make it clear that the Lord does not cause people to do evil, and the phrase *gave them up* thus cannot mean that these people could not choose otherwise or repent once they sinned. This is reinforced by the meaning of *knowledge* in the phrase *retain God in their knowledge* (see above). Paul seems to be relying on the Old Testament literary convention of ascribing all actions to God's power, though his usage is different. The phrase *gave them up* is considerably less forceful than *caused* or *hardened*. Paul's use of this convention indicates his familiarity with the Old Testament and does not imply a lack of free agency, as the Old Testament use might if not understood.

> Being filled with all unrighteousness, fornication, wickedness, covetousness, maliciousness; full of envy, murder, debate, deceit, malignity; whisperers, Backbiters, haters of God, despiteful, proud, boasters, inventors of evil things, disobedient to parents, Without understanding, covenantbreakers, without natural affection, implacable, unmerciful:

Mind

The Greek word *nous* (νοῦς), translated "mind," means something broader than our concept of mind. For the Greeks of Paul's time, *mind* referred to the totality of both moral and mental existence. For us, the word *mind* refers almost exclusively to consciousness, although that way of understanding *mind* is relatively recent, perhaps no earlier than the seventeenth century. Anciently *mind* could include "insight," "inventiveness," "disposition," and "character."[115] Paul says that idolaters are immoral and their reasonings are vain (see verse 21) because they have unfit minds. Good thinking and morality cannot be separated.

They did not like to retain God in their knowledge . . . [so] God gave them over to a reprobate mind

The alternate translation of the phrase *they did not like to retain God in their knowledge . . . [so] God gave them over to a reprobate mind* shows a wordplay Paul uses to make a point: "They did not think it *fit to* [*dokimazō*, δοκιμάζω] . . . [so] he left them to an *unfit* [*adokimos*, ἀδόκιμος] mind." This is a variation of verse 24 and helps us understand that the "reward" of sin is to be given over to it. Because these sinners did not think it appropriate to concern themselves with understanding God, who is ultimately the supreme thing worth understanding, the Father allowed them to have inappropriate, unfit, and worthless minds. Such minds are not suited to understanding him. God gave them what they demanded: minds not fitted to him. (Recall from the discussion of truth, verse 18, pages 73–75, what it means for them not to be fitted to, in other words, not in harmony with, the truth.)

Not convenient

As the alternate translation shows, in modern usage "convenient" is not a sufficiently strong translation, though in the etymology of *convenient* we see that its roots mean "that which comes together." The Greek word for *convenient* is *kathēkontōs* (καθηκόντως). In Stoic philosophy it means "what is in accord with duty."[116] The point is that the Romans do not do what they are supposed to do.

JST Verse 28

> And even as they did not like to retain God <u>according to some</u> knowledge, God gave them over to a reprobate mind, to do the those things which are not convenient.

It is not clear what to make of Joseph Smith's changing *in their knowledge* to *according to some knowledge*, because it is not clear what the changed phrase means. One possibility is that the Prophet's view of the world is different from Paul's. Paul clearly believes that everyone comes into the world knowing of God. It is not apparent just what that means or in what way they know, but it is evident that Paul holds the view that everyone knows of God in some way. On the other hand, the Prophet Joseph may be suggesting that some simply do not know of God. If a knowledge of God is something learned from culture, tradition, and family, then it is quite conceivable that not all have that knowledge. The Book of Mormon's insistence on the importance of the brass plates, record keeping, and preaching seems to be in agreement with the latter view.

Verses 29–31

In verses 29–31, Paul gives a comprehensive list of sins. Notice that the list contains three sublists: (1) being filled with all unrighteousness, fornication, wickedness, covetousness, maliciousness; (2) full of envy, murder, debate, deceit, malignity; and (3) whisperers, backbiters, haters of God, despiteful, proud, boasters, inventors of evil things, disobedient to parents, without understanding, covenant-breakers, without natural affection, implacable, unmerciful.

Some have asserted that the order of the lists is meaningful, but this requires a good deal of straining. Paul may be listing four general types of sin—fornication, wickedness, covetousness, and maliciousness (see verse 29)—and then giving specific examples of these general types. However, he appears simply to be giving a long list of possible sins, running the gamut from what we might think of as small, like gossiping, to great, like murder. The order seems to be a function of the sounds of the Greek words, especially in the first two lists, where Paul groups words with similar endings, prefixes, or other sounds. For example, the sins mentioned in verse 31 all begin with the Greek letter alpha. It is not possible to effectively translate this rhetorical ordering into English.

The effect of a long list like this is much more powerful than the phrase *many sins* would be, especially when the words are also joined by similar sounds. Paul is obviously interested in using language to best present his message to his listeners: he wants them not only to hear the doctrinal content of his message (which could be stated, perhaps, in a chapter or two), but also to feel what he is saying. However, unlike the sophist or the con artist, Paul uses language that matches its content. He uses rhetoric not in place of content, but as part of it.

Filled

The Greek word translated "filled" (*plēroō*, πληρόω) is a perfect passive participle. The translation is thus "being filled" or "having been filled." The perfect tense indicates completion or fullness, so we might translate this as "having been completely filled" or "having already been completely filled." Those of whom Paul speaks here, namely, sinners, are completely unrighteous. Being unrighteous is ultimately not a matter of degree; one either is or is not unrighteous.

Unrighteousness

Unrighteousness could also be translated "injustice." (See the discussion of *ungodliness and unrighteousness* in verse 18, page 73.)

Fornication

The sin of fornication is not mentioned in every New Testament manuscript; in fact, many of the better manuscripts leave it out. The Greek word for *fornication* or *prostitution* (*porneia*, πορνεία [one of the roots of our word *pornography*]) and the word for *malice* (*ponēria*, πονερία) look much alike, and there appears to have been some confusion of the text by transcribers. That may explain why it appears in some manuscripts and not in others. The word translated "fornication" includes all sexual sin.[117]

Covetousness

The alternate translation uses "insatiability" rather than "covetousness" to remind us of what it means to be covetous. Covetousness is having inappropriate desires, desires not contained within proper bounds. Understanding the New Testament notion of perfection and the necessity of bounds or limits (see pages 12–13, 15–23) suggests that desires that remain within their proper boundaries are perfect. It also suggests that we may be able

> Who knowing the judgment of God, that they which commit such things are worthy of death, not only do the same, but have pleasure in them that do them.

to think of all imperfection as a kind of covetousness, desiring to go beyond the bounds appropriate to one's existence.

Malignity

"Evil habits" or "craftiness," indicating guile and machination, are variations of the word translated "malignity." The alternate translation uses "conspiracy."

Whisperers

Whisperers are those who spread gossip.

Backbiters

Backbiters are slanderers.

Despiteful

The Greek word *hubristēs* (ὑβριστής), translated "despiteful," could also be translated "hubristic." In the New Testament, it often means something like "arrogant" or "insolent" and can also mean "insulting."[118] *Hubristēs* describes one who cannot be governed, so it may be an implicit reference to those who refuse their service to God. To help distinguish this sin from pride, the alternate translation harks back to the earlier meaning of the word, "those who go beyond the mark" (compare Jacob 4:14). This earlier meaning explains what it means to be arrogant.

Proud

Proud could be translated "arrogant." This pride is not positive. In fact, though the English scriptures use the word *pride* and variations of it 184 times, as Ezra Taft Benson pointed out, there is not one scriptural use of it as a positive attribute. [119]

Latter-day scripture is especially adamant

that pride is not good. The Book of Mormon discusses pride considerably more than do the other scriptures, referring to it at least sixty-nine times, mostly in the writings before Christ (fifty-eight times). According to a WordCruncher™ analysis, the Book of Mormon uses *pride* 16 percent more often than one would expect if the words of scripture were randomly distributed. This is an indication of its importance to Book of Mormon writers. To my knowledge, not once does the Book of Mormon speak of pride positively. These facts should give us pause when we talk about a positive kind of pride. We might ask ourselves, "What is the scriptural term for that?" If there is one, it might be helpful to use it, and that might help us avoid viewing as positive something the scriptures universally condemn.

Without understanding

Verses 19–23 have shown how people have become without understanding, in other words, undiscerning.

Implacable

The Greek word translated "implacable" (*aspondos*, ἄσπονδος), meaning "irreconcilable," is not included in the better manuscripts. Modern editors usually omit it from the text.

JST Verses 29–31

No change.

Verse 32

This is the end of the sentence that began in verse 28. Paul again uses the rhetorical device of inclusion (see the discussion of verse 25, page 87). In verse 28 he described people who did not think a knowledge of God was fit to keep in their minds (or, as we might say, in their hearts). This is the first part of the inclusion and will be repeated at the end. The center portion is in verses 29–31, where Paul enumerated the ways in which these people were unfit, or the sins the Lord allowed them to be given over to. In verse 32, he concludes the inclusion by referring to the sinners in verse 28 and their fitness of mind in knowing of the judgment and justice of God. They know that what they do is wrong, but they not only do those things, they also take pleasure in seeing others do them. A diagram of this inclusion follows:

> They did not like to retain God in their knowledge, so he gave them over to their unfit minds and their sinning (verse 28)
>> They were unrighteous, fornicators, iniquitous, covetous, malicious; full of envy. . . . (verses 29–31)
> They knew that these things were worthy of death, but did them anyway and took pleasure in seeing others do them (verse 32)

In this context, retaining God in their knowledge and knowing that these things are worthy of death are the same: sinners know they are worthy of death if they retain a knowledge of God. They deceive themselves, not liking to retain a knowledge of God but knowing nonetheless that the result of doing such things is death, be it physical or spiritual. The idea that the Father turns them over to their unfit minds and the idea that they take pleasure in the sinning of others are thus also parallel. Their pleasure in the sins of others is perfect evidence of their unfit minds.

Judgment

The Greek word translated "judgment," *dikaiōma* (δικαίωμα), is related to the word translated elsewhere as "righteousness" and "justice" (see the discussion of *righteousness of God* in verse 17, pages 58–63). There are two ways to understand the word *judgment*. One way is to see it as a use of legal language: God has pronounced the verdict of guilty on those who sin, and these people, though they

understand that verdict and its sentence of death, not only do the things that will bring the sentence upon them, but also take pleasure in seeing others do them.

The other way to understand the word *judgment* results from the fact that the word translated "judgment" often refers to the rules and regulations that maintain harmony.[120] Given this information, we could also translate it "commandment" or "regulation." The Greek word does not commit Paul to either meaning, leaving both open for his listeners to hear (the two are obviously related). English does not allow the same richness of meaning. The alternate translation arbitrarily uses the first of these meanings, but the second is equally acceptable.

Knowing the judgment of God

Paul has already explained how the sinners know God (see verses 19 and 20) even though they have deceived themselves into thinking that they do not know him. In the phrase *knowing the judgment of God*, Paul says that sinners implicitly understand God's sentence on those who commit the sins he has listed.

Worthy of death

Worthy of death could also be translated "liable to death." Perhaps to some readers' surprise, not only are murder and unchastity said to warrant death, but so are whispering (gossiping) and pride. As becomes clear at the beginning of chapter 2, Paul expects those who hear or read this list to be smug, looking condescendingly at the people he describes as they agree with Paul that those people really are evil. We may be tempted to the same condescension as we read verses 22–27. As a result, we may assume that Paul means that one who commits these sins is worthy of capital punishment, but when we look closer at the range of sins that he has introduced, we

> Who knowing the judgment of God, that they which commit such things are worthy of death, not only do the same, but have pleasure in them that do them.

have to question whether the word *death* really means "capital punishment." One explanation is that Paul is using hyperbole, or exaggeration, to achieve the effect he desires. Another likely explanation is that he means that those who do these things are worthy of spiritual death. Since no unclean thing can enter the kingdom of heaven, those who commit such sins are worthy of being, or liable to be, cut off from the presence of God. Paul may also mean that the sins he lists make us worthy of physical death. Those who commit them should not be executed, but because of sins we suffer physical death. In other places it appears that Paul may believe that we die not only because of Adam's transgression, but because of our own sins as well (see Romans 5:12 and 1 Corinthians 15:21; compare Moses 6:48).

The comparison of verses 1–17 with verses 18–32 draws our attention to the emphasis in the latter section on the fact that sin brings spiritual death. The first verses of Romans 1 are about the gospel and Paul's preaching of it. In Greek, the last word of verse 17 is *life*, referring to eternal life. Verses 18–32 are about those who have been disobedient. Though it is not the last word, death is referred to at the end of this section. The central contrast in these two sections, then, is between the life brought by the gospel and the death brought by the denial of God, by disobedience. Romans 1 parallels the first two divisions of the entire letter to the Romans (see the discussion of *the just shall live by faith* in verse 17, pages 67–70, as well as the outline of the book, pages xx–xxi).

Because Paul discussed the content of the gospel in terms of the relation between the spirit and the flesh, and because he used Christ's resurrection from the dead as his example of God's power (see verses 3 and 4), we can view the rest of the chapter as a working out of that theme. Obedience to the gospel brings life, which is the union of spirit and flesh and the overcoming of sin (see verses 4–17). On the other hand, sin brings death, which is the dissolution of the spirit and the destruction of one's body by lust (see verses 18–32).

Not only do the same, but have pleasure in them that do them

As the alternate translation shows, the sense of *not only do the same, but have pleasure in them that do them* seems to be that those who sin approve of the sins of others. Perhaps they encourage them. Perhaps they excuse them. Perhaps some even take pleasure in seeing others join them in sin. Sometimes we sin without recommending our sin to others. Even though we act unrighteously, we at least say that we do not want others to do what we have done. However, the people Paul is discussing not only sin, they also approve of the fact that others sin, even knowing, by the light of Christ, that what they are doing is wrong.

Though it may seem unlikely, I believe it is impossible to sin without recommending our sins to others in some sense. When I sin, I do what I sincerely believe to be wrong. If that were not true, although what I do might be a mistake, it seems odd to call it a sin. If I do what I believe to be wrong, I must in some way or another convince myself that it is either right or inescapable. Otherwise, I would do what I believe to be right. In other words, I must have and believe reasons, even deceptive excuses, for my behavior when I sin. Sin is always a form of self-deception. That I always recommend my sins to others follows from this conclusion. Any reasons to commit sin would also be reasons for another to do the same thing in my situation. If they are not sufficient for someone else in my situation, then they are not sufficient for me. Regardless of what I say to others or to myself, when I sin I implicitly recommend my sins to anyone in my situation. Conversely, I necessarily approve of the sins of others whenever I myself sin.

JST Verse 32

And some who, knowing the judgment of God, that they which commit such things are worthy of death, are inexcusable, not only do the same, but have pleasure in them that do them.

The addition of *are inexcusable* in the inspired translation redescribes those who know the judgment of God. The King James translation of the Greek text says that some not only sin, but take pleasure in the fact that others sin. It parenthetically remarks that those who do this know that God considers them worthy of death. The Prophet's addition changes the parenthetical clause, indicating that sinners know that God thinks them worthy of death and adding that they have no excuse. Joseph Smith's change in this verse connects it to verse 20, making the last part of the chapter a sort of inclusion or, perhaps, a very loose chiasm:

A   Idolaters are without excuse because they understand "from the creation" (verse 20)

    B   How their refusal to know God made them idolaters (verses 21–26)

    B'   A list of sins along with a repetition in verse 28 of the problem that occasions those sins (verses 26–31)

A'   A return, not only to verse 28 (as in the Greek and King James texts), but also to verse 20 (verse 32)

It may be possible to think of the two center parts of this inclusion (verses 21–26 and 26–31) as parallel to each other: the sins listed in verses 29–31 result from the same kind of refusal to know God that also brings about idolatry. They are the same kind of act, a turning away from God toward something else, usually one's own will. If this parallel is valid, this may, very loosely, be a chiasm. Chiasmus and inclusion may overlap.

NOTES

1. As noted in the introduction, the alternate translation is one I have composed using *The Greek New Testament*, 4th ed., rev. (Stuttgart: United Bible Societies, 1993).

2. See, for example, William G. Doty, *Letters in Primitive Christianity* (Philadelphia: Fortress Press, 1973), 27–31.

3. See Dale B. Martin, *Slavery as Salvation: The Metaphor of Slavery in Pauline Christianity* (New Haven, Conn.: Yale University Press, 1990), 33.

4. See Walter Bauer, *A Greek-English Lexicon of the New Testament and Other Early Christian Literature*, trans. William F. Arndt and F. Wilbur Gingrich, 2nd ed. rev. (Chicago: University of Chicago Press, 1979), 637.

5. For example, Roman slavery seems not usually to have broken up families in the way that American slavery did. See Martin, *Slavery as Salvation*, 3.

6. See Zvi Yavetz, *Slaves and Slavery in Ancient Rome* (New Brunswick, N.J.: Transaction Books, 1988), 1; Mary Ann Beavis, "Ancient Slavery as an Interpretive Context for the New Testament Servant Parables with Special Reference to the Unjust Steward (Luke 16:1–8)," *Journal of Biblical Literature* 3/1 (1992): 39.

7. See K. R. Bradley, *Slaves and Masters in the Roman Empire: A Study in Social Control* (Brussels: Latomus Revue d'Études Latines, 1984), 18–20, 139–40.

8. See Martin, *Slavery as Salvation*, xvi.

9. See Muhammad A. Dandamayev, "Slavery: Ancient Near East," in *Anchor Bible Dictionary*, ed. David Noel Freedman (New York: Doubleday, 1992), 6:58–62.

10. See Gerhard Kittel, ed., *Theological Dictionary of the New Testament* (Grand Rapids, Mich.: Eerdmans, 1964–74), 2:261, 266.

11. See also Matthew 21:33–41; 22:1–14; 24:45–51; Luke 2:29; Acts 2:18; 4:29; 16:17; 1 Peter 2:16.

12. See Martin, *Slavery as Salvation*, 51–52.

13. See Kittel, *Theological Dictionary*, 2:271.

14. See ibid., 2:271–72.

15. See Martin, *Slavery as Salvation*, 49, 51.

16. Epictetus, *Discourses* 4.1.62–64.

17. Ibid., 4.1.1–3.

18. The shock may have been lessened by the fact that Greeks and Greek-speaking people could also think of a king or other leader as a slave (see Martin, *Slavery as Salvation*, 86–88). However, that seems not to be the way that Paul is using the

term, for rather than speaking of himself as one enslaved by his people and responsibilities, he speaks of himself as enslaved by Jesus Christ.

19. I take it that this is Hugh W. Nibley's point in "Work We Must but the Lunch Is Free," in *Approaching Zion* (Salt Lake City: Deseret Book and FARMS, 1989), 202–51.

20. For a brief overview of the history of the self and some criticisms of the contemporary view of the self, see James E. Faulconer and Richard N. Williams, "Reconsidering Psychology," in *Reconsidering Psychology: Perspectives from Continental Philosophy*, ed. James E. Faulconer and Richard N. Williams (Pittsburgh: Duquesne University Press, 1990), 9–60.

21. Also notice that the next verse (1 Corinthians 9:17) makes clear that Paul does not do his own will but the will of another, and that doing so marks his work as a stewardship, or *oikonomia* (οἰκονομία; translated "dispensation" in the KJV), that has been entrusted to him, rather than a paid job. The steward, or *oikonomos* (οἰκονόμος), is the slave who manages or rules the affairs of the household, or *oikos* (οἶκος). For more on stewardship and the use of that idea in early Christianity, see Martin, *Slavery as Salvation*, 15–22.

22. Elder Neal A. Maxwell agrees with Paul rather than with contemporary culture: "The submission of one's will is placing on God's altar the only uniquely personal thing one has to place there" (Neal A. Maxwell, *If Thou Endure It Well* [Salt Lake City: Bookcraft, 1996], 54). As Michael Wyschogrod says, "A slave who is totally enslaved is an inanimate object" (as quoted in André LaCocque and Paul Ricoeur, *Thinking Biblically: Exegetical and Hermeneutical Studies*, trans. David Pellauer [Chicago: University of Chicago Press, 1998], 73). As André LaCocque says, "The Bible emphasizes the 'need for a *continual* surrender of autonomy,'" something that requires one's will (ibid.).

23. See Frederich W. Knobloch, "Adoption," in *Anchor Bible Dictionary*, 1:78; Joseph A. Fitzmyer, *Romans: A New Translation with Introduction and Commentary*, The Anchor Bible, vol. 33 (New York: Doubleday, 1993), 499–500.

24. See Bauer, *Greek-English Lexicon*, 604.

25. In contrast, Israelite fathers seem not to have had the absolute authority that other ancient fathers had. Though children were considered property, Deuteronomy 21:18–21 shows that a father's power over his children (at least over his sons) was sometimes limited and required court approval. See Christopher J. H. Wright, "Family," in *Anchor Bible Dictionary*, 2:767.

26. See Beavis, "Ancient Slavery as an Interpretive Context," 37; Bradley, *Slaves and Masters*, 19. Note, too, that besides kindness and custom, there were economic incentives for masters to treat their slaves kindly. It makes no sense to abuse or destroy valuable property. Evidence suggests that masters might manumit slaves to control their other slaves better by holding out the hope of manumission and also to gain social and political advantages among their peers. See Bradley, *Slaves and Masters*, 21–22.

27. See Martin, *Slavery as Salvation*, xix, 60–68.

28. See ibid., 15–22.

29. It may seem that we do, indeed, choose another master if we choose to follow Satan. However, since his claim to mastery is at best temporary and ultimately illegitimate, if we choose to follow him, we really only refuse our real master, the Father. Perhaps that is why sons of perdition become masters of Satan rather than the reverse. See Moses 5:23, where Cain is told that he will rule over Satan. To choose to follow Satan is to choose against divine mastery and the order that follows from mastery and to choose mere chaos instead.

30. See Salo Wittmayer Baron, *A Social and Religious History of the Jews*, 2nd ed. rev. (New York: Columbia University Press, 1952), 1:73–81, 149–51; E. Mary Smallwood, "High Priests and Politics in Roman Palestine," *Journal of Theological Studies* 13 (1962): 14–34.

31. It is worth considering the connection between the use of the word *anointing* in the Old and New Testaments and its use in the latter days, and it may be especially fruitful to consider the connection between ancient and modern anointings and Jesus' title the Anointed One.

32. See A. T. Robertson, *A Grammar of the*

Greek New Testament in the Light of Historical Research (Nashville: Broadman, 1934), 496.

33. See Kittel, *Theological Dictionary*, 1:414–19.

34. See ibid., 9:12–13.

35. Perhaps one aspect of the Word of Wisdom is its typological identification with the Nazarite vow, as well as with the fact that the Savior will refrain from drinking wine until he can drink it again with the saints (see Matthew 26:29; Mark 14:25; Luke 22:18; D&C 27:3–5; 89:5).

36. For example, see Aristotle's discussion of essence in *Posterior Analytics* 73a35–b24 and, especially, *Metaphysics* 1022a14–36.

37. See Bauer, *Greek-English Lexicon*, 317; Kittel, *Theological Dictionary*, 2:724.

38. Deuteronomy 6:4; see 5:1; 9:1; 20:3; 32:1; Judges 5:3; Psalms 50:7; 81:8; Proverbs 4:10; Isaiah 1:2; 44:1; Jeremiah 6:19; Daniel 9:19; as well as a related idea in latter-day scripture, such as D&C 41:1; 76:1; 109:78; 133:16.

39. Psalm 118:25–26; Matthew 21:9; 23:39; Mark 11:9; Luke 13:35; compare 1 Nephi 11:6 and especially 3 Nephi 4:32; 11:17; D&C 19:37; 36:3; 39:19; 109:79; 124:101.

40. See Kittel, *Theological Dictionary*, 2:729–35.

41. This emphasis on the activity of preaching rather than the content of preaching is something that marks Christian self-understanding until approximately the time of the Reformation. For more on this, see my "Scripture as Incarnation," forthcoming in *Historicity and the Latter-day Saint Scriptures*, ed. Paul Y. Hoskisson (Provo, Utah: BYU Religious Studies Center, 2000).

42. See D&C 1:28; 4:6; 19:21–23; 46:18; 50:40; 88:78–80; 93:24; 130:19; 131:6; 132:24.

43. For more about the importance of preaching and hearing, see 1 Corinthians 1:18 and such Book of Mormon passages as Alma 53:10 and Helaman 3:29. For additional Old Testament background on the belief in the power of God's word itself and not just the meaning found in that word, see passages such as Genesis 1:3; Psalm 147:15; Isaiah 40:8; 55:10–11; Jeremiah 23:29. See also passages such as 3 Nephi 28:20 and 4 Nephi 1:30.

44. See Fitzmyer, *Romans: A New Translation*, 232.

45. As noted in the introduction, words in the JST that have been added to the KJV or changed in some way are underlined, and deletions are marked by two slashes (//) at the point of the deletion.

46. It is also probably true that because the people of Paul's day could not depend on written texts, they were good listeners and good at remembering what they heard. Plato's *Phaedrus* points out that writing robs us of our memory (see 274e–275b, especially 275a).

47. For an excellent discussion of various kinds of knowledge, kinds that cannot be reduced to or modeled on scientific knowledge, see Aristotle's *Nichomachean Ethics*, 1139b14–1143b17, also 1094b12–27. For a contemporary discussion of many of the issues, see Hans-Georg Gadamer, *Truth and Method*, trans. Joel Weinsheimer and Donald Marshall, 2nd ed. rev. (New York: Continuum, 1993).

48. Wisdom is part of what we commonly call the Apocrypha, but because Joseph Smith said that these works contain much in them that is for our profit and that we should read them with a discerning spirit (see D&C 91), we might do better to call them the deuterocanonical works, as others do who think of them as at least partly inspired but not on par with the scriptures. *Deuterocanonical* means that they are secondary in importance to the canonized works, the scriptures.

49. See Rudolph Bultmann, *Theology of the New Testament*, trans. Kendrick Gobel (New York: Charles Scribner's Sons, 1951–55), 2:121.

50. See C. E. B. Cranfield, *A Critical and Exegetical Commentary on the Epistle to the Romans*, 6th ed. (Edinburgh: T & T Clark, 1975–79), 1:58.

51. Some understand Philippians 2:5–9 to teach that Christ *became* the Son of God through his ministry. Though there is not space here to deal with the issue fully, suffice it to say that latter-day revelation teaches otherwise.

52. See Fitzmyer, *Romans: A New Translation*, 112.

53. This should make it more clear why most non–Latter-day Saint Christians are scandalized by Latter-day Saint belief. They believe we implicitly deny the atonement when we believe that the

gap between the human and the divine can be crossed by the human's becoming divine. They do not understand that humans can become divine only because the Son first crosses that gap and then brings us across to him. They also do not understand that to become divine is *not* to become equal to God.

54. See Fitzmyer, *Romans: A New Translation,* 234.

55. See Cranfield, *Critical and Exegetical Commentary,* 1:59.

56. For example, see Aristotle's discussion of essence in *Posterior Analytics* 73a35–b24 and, especially, *Metaphysics* 1022a14–36.

57. Similarly, "the fundamental verbal tense of the Decalogue is the indicative present, and the negation—that precedes most of the Ten Words [i.e., the Ten Commandments]—does not introduce a prohibition (*ʾal*), but an ordinary statement in the indicative (*loʾ*)" (LaCocque and Ricoeur, *Thinking Biblically,* 85).

58. See Fitzmyer, *Romans: A New Translation,* 235.

59. The first examination of chiasmus in scripture by a Latter-day Saint was by John W. Welch. See his "Chiasmus in the Book of Mormon," *BYU Studies* 10/1 (1969): 69–84.

60. See Kittel, *Theological Dictionary,* 9:373; Bauer, *Greek-English Lexicon,* 877.

61. See Bauer, *Greek-English Lexicon,* 662; Kittel, *Theological Dictionary,* 6:175–77, 203–4.

62. See Kittel, *Theological Dictionary,* 1:36.

63. See ibid., 1:11, 88–97.

64. See Robert D. Haak, "Altar," in *Anchor Bible Dictionary,* 1:162–65, for a discussion of altar use in Israel.

65. See Fitzmyer, *Romans: A New Translation,* 228

66. See Robertson, *Grammar of the Greek New Testament,* 962, 1189–90.

67. See *Oxford English Dictionary,* 2nd ed., s.v. "keep"; *American Dictionary of the English Language* (1828), s.v. "keep."

68. See Bauer, *Greek-English Lexicon,* 323.

69. See Ibid., 768.

70. Many have come to this conclusion by assuming that Sarah's death, mentioned early in Genesis 23, occurred shortly after the sacrifice at Mount Moriah and subtracting her age at Isaac's birth from her age at death.

71. See Fitzmyer, *Romans: A New Translation,* 249.

72. See Kittel, *Theological Dictionary,* 3:615; Bauer, *Greek-English Lexicon,* 404–5.

73. See Kittel, *Theological Dictionary,* 7:965.

74. See Bauer, *Greek-English Lexicon,* 196.

75. See John Murray, *The Epistle to the Romans* (Grand Rapids, Mich.: Eerdmans, 1959), 1:30.

76. Murray shares this view rather than the common Protestant view that he mentions earlier. See ibid., 1:30–31.

77. See Kittel, *Theological Dictionary* 1:179–80, 184, 188.

78. See Fitzmyer, *Romans: A New Translation,* 257.

79. See LaCocque and Ricouer, *Thinking Biblically,* 71–109 (especially 82–95), 111–38.

80. However, the Father *is* fair in some circumstances. After all, if we do not forgive, then we will not be forgiven. That is a description of fairness.

81. Psalm 137 is one example of such a remonstration or lament, as is Abraham's argument with God in Genesis 18:20–33. See Graham S. Ogden, "Joel 4 and Prophetic Responses to National Laments," *Journal for the Study of the Old Testament* 26 (June 1983), 97–106; "Prophetic Oracles against Foreign Nations and Psalms of Communal Lament: The Relationship of Psalm 137 to Jeremiah 49:7–22 and Obadiah," *Journal for the Study of the Old Testament* 24 (October 1982): 89–97.

82. For example, see Cranfield, *Critical and Exegetical Commentary,* 1:102.

83. See ibid., 1:103.

84. Fitzmyer attributes this interpretation to Ramaroson (see Fitzmyer, *Romans: A New Translation,* 263).

85. See Kittel, *Theological Dictionary,* 2:188–90.

86. See Romans 2:7; 4:17; 5:10, 17, 18, 21; 6:2, 4, 10, 11, 13, 22, 23; 7:1, 2, 3, 9, 10; 8:2, 6, 11, 12, 13, 38; 9:26; 10:5; 11:15; 12:1; 14:7, 8, 9, 11. Also recall the major divisions of the letter (see pages xx–xxi).

87. See Matthew 5:3, 5, 7, 9, 10–12, 21–25, 27–28, 38–48; 6:14–15, 19–21; 7:1–5; 3 Nephi 12:3, 5, 7, 9, 10–12, 21–26, 27–30, 38–48; 13:14–15, 19–21; 14:1–5.

88. See Fitzmyer, *Romans: A New Translation,* 265.

89. "The Talmud records the famous remark of R. Simlai (Makkot 23b), 'Moses gave Israel 613 commandments. David reduced them to 10, Isaiah to 2, but Habakkuk to one: *the righteous shall live by his faith*'" (A. Cohen, ed., *The Twelve Prophets: Hebrew Text, English Translation and Commentary* [London: Soncino Press, 1959], 219).

90. See Cranfield, *Critical and Exegetical Commentary,* 1:102.

91. Perhaps Cranfield's commitment to evangelical Protestant doctrine explains his emphasis on the first two sections and his neglect of the third.

92. The Greek word *asebeia* literally means "failure to worship," but in general usage it has a more narrow character: not just failure to worship, but failure to recognize God. See Romans 11:26; 2 Timothy 2:16; Titus 2:12; Jude 1:15, 18 for other uses of the term, as well as related terms in 1 Peter 4:18; 2 Peter 2:5–6; 3:7; Jude 1:4; 4:5; 5:6.

93. See Plato, *Meno,* passim, and *Republic,* book 7.

94. Thorlief Boman, *Hebrew Thought Compared with Greek* (Philadelphia: Westminster Press, 1961), 45.

95. Ibid., 45–46

96. For more on the question of how the ancients understand the real, see James E. Faulconer, *Scripture Study: Tools and Suggestions* (Provo, Utah: FARMS, 1999), 123–53; and "Scripture as Incarnation."

97. See Kittel, *Theological Dictionary,* 1:238, where it is discussed as "nonconcealment"; Henry G. Liddell and Robert Scott, comps., *Greek-English Lexicon* (Oxford: Clarendon, 1968), 63–64.

98. We see evidence of this understanding of knowledge as acquaintance in the story of Adam and Eve in the Garden of Eden. We also see it in Plato, for example, in his story of how we came to know the Forms (the ultimate reality of things) in a preexistent life where we were acquainted with them.

99. See Bauer, *Greek-English Lexicon,* 164.

100. For example, Stoic philosophy speaks of the state of being in the truth, that is, knowing the truth, as harmony or imperturbability. See Ioannes ab Arnim, comp., *Stoicorum Veterum Fragmenta* (Stuttgart: B. G. Teubner, 1964), 1:49–55.

101. Again, Stoic philosophy provides an excellent example. For an excellent, brief article on stoicism, see Thomas Schmeller, "Stoicism," in *Anchor Bible Dictionary,* 6:210–14.

102. See Bauer, *Greek-English Lexicon,* 87; Fitzmyer, *Romans: A New Translation,* 280.

103. See Kittel, *Theological Dictionary,* 2:285.

104. See Matthew 15:19; Mark 7:21; Luke 24:38; Romans 14:1; 1 Corinthians 3:20; Philippians 2:14; 1 Timothy 2:8; James 2:4. Some uses of the word in Luke may not be negative (see 2:35; 5:22; 6:8; 9:46, 47), but the context of those uses and the fact that the word is negative in every other case suggests that it should be read as a negative term in those verses too.

105. See T. F. Glasson, "'Visions of thy Head' (Daniel 2^{28}): The Heart and the Head in Bible Psychology," *The Expository Times* 81/8 (May 1970): 247–48.

106. For the other uses of the word, see Mark 14:61; Luke 1:68; Romans 9:5; 2 Corinthians 1:3; 11:31; Ephesians 1:3; 1 Peter 1:3.

107. See Kittel, *Theological Dictionary,* 1:335–36.

108. This discussion of need and desire is consequent on my understanding of Emmanual Levinas's discussion of them in *Totality and Infinity: An Essay on Exteriority,* trans. Alphonso Lingis (Pittsburgh: Duquesne University Press, 1969), 104, 117, 179, 236, 254–73.

109. Paul also uses this word in Romans 2:9; 4:15; 5:3; 7:8, 13, 15, 17, 18, 20; 15:18.

110. See Bauer, *Greek-English Lexicon,* 421.

111. It is interesting that the steward is rewarded. Reward is commensurate with service to God, though we do not *earn* whatever reward we may receive. See also Mosiah 2:21; Matthew 20:1–16.

112. See Liddell and Scott, *Greek-English Lexicon,* 205.

113. Bauer, *Greek-English Lexicon*, 75.

114. Most modern translations deal with this literary convention by translating it in the active voice or by leaving the subject indefinite. For example, we see these varying translations of the phrase in Exodus 7:13: "Pharaoh's heart was hard" (M. Rosenbaum and A. M. Silbermann, trans., *Pentateuch with Rashi's Commentary* [London: Shapiro, Vallentine, 1945], 1:31) and "Pharaoh, however, remained obstinate" (*The New Jerusalem Bible: Reader's Edition* [New York: Doubleday, 1990]).

115. See Kittel, *Theological Dictionary*, 4:952–53.

116. See Bauer, *Greek-English Lexicon*, 389. For example, see Polybius, *Histories* 6.6.1–8. Incidentally, though *kathekontos* is not related to the word translated "fit" in the alternate translation, "fitting" is a good translation here.

117. See Bauer, *Greek-English Lexicon*, 693.

118. See Ibid., 832.

119. See Ezra Taft Benson, "Beware of Pride," *Ensign*, May 1989, 4–7.

120. See Bauer, *Greek-English Lexicon*, 198; Kittel, *Theological Dictionary*, 2:219–23.

CITATION INDEX

INDEX OF GREEK AND HEBREW TERMS

erōs (ἔρως) "love," 34
euangelion (εὐαγγέλιον) "gospel; good news; pleasing message; goodness," 13–14, 16
eucharisteō (εὐχαριστέω) "thank," 40, 82
eulogētos (εὐλογητός) "is blessed," 88
euodoō (εὐοδόω) "to have a prosperous journey," 44

gar (γάρ) "for," 42
gignomai (γίγνομαι) "made," 20
gnōstos (γνωστός) "knowledge; understanding," 76, 81
goy qadosh (גּוֹי קָדוֹשׁ) "nation of saints," 35

hagios (ἅγιος) "holy; saint; one of God's people," 25, 34, 35
hagiōsunēs (ἁγιωσύνης) "of holiness," 25
hebel (הֶבֶל) "vain things," 82
horizō (ὁρίζω) "declared," 21, 23
hubristēs (ὑβριστής) "spiteful; despiteful," 94
huios (υἱός) "son," 18

kata (κάτα) "according to," 24
katechō (κατέχω) "hold; to hold captive," 75
katergazdomai (κατεργάζομαι) "working," 89
kathēkontōs (καθηκόντως) "convenient; fitting," 92, 104n. 116
klētos (κλήτος) "called," 10
kosmos (κόσμος) "world," 78

latreuō (λατρεύω) "served; service to the gods; worship," 42, 88
loʾ (statement in the indicative), 102n. 57

martus (μάρτυς) "witness," 42
mataioō (ματαιόω) "vain," 82
mōrainō (μωραίνω) "became fools," 85
morphē (μορφή) "form," 8

nous (νοῦς) "mind," 92

oikonomia (οἰκονομία) "dispensation," 100n. 21
oikonomos (οἰκονόμος) "steward," 100n. 21
oikos (οἶκος) "household," 100n. 21
orgē (ὀργή) "wrath," 72

pais (παῖς) "child (son); slave," 7
paradidōmi (παραδίδωμι) "gave them up," 86
paraklētos (παράκλητος) "the comforter," 10
Paulos (Παῦλος) "Paul," 3
phaneroō (φανερόω) "hath shewed; revealed," 77
phaneros (φανερός) "manifest," 76–77
phthartos (φθαρτός) "corruptible; mortal," 83

pisteuō (πιστεύω) "believeth," 57
pistis (πίστις) "faith; trust," 31, 57
planē aōtōn (πλάνη αὠτῶν) "their deceit of themselves," 90
pleroō (πληρόω) "filled," 93
pneuma (πνεῦμα) "spirit," 24, 42, 46
pneuma hagion (πνεῦμα ἅγιον) "Holy Spirit; spirit of holiness," 25
pneuma hagiōsunēs (πνεῦμα ἁγιωσύνης) "spirit of holiness," 25. *See also* hagios
ponēria (πονερία) "malice," 93
porneia (πορνεία) "fornication; prostitution," 93
proepangellō (προεπαγγέλλω) "promised," 16
prophētēs (προφήτης) "an interpreter," 16
pseudei (Ψεύδει) "lie," 87

qodesh (קֹדֶשׁ) "holy," 34

ruach qadosh (רוּחַ קָדֹשׁ) "spirit of holiness," 25

sebazomai (σεβάζομαι) "worshipped," 87
shaliyha (שָׁלִיחַ) "apostle," 11
sōtērion (σωτήριον) "rescue from evil or harm," 55–57
stērizō (στηρίζω) "established," 47
sumparakaleō (συμπαρακαλέω) "comfort," 47

theotes (θεότης) "divinity; Godhead," 80
tsdq (צדק) "holy," 60

zaō (ζάω) "live," 66

Subject Index

THE FOUNDATION FOR ANCIENT RESEARCH AND MORMON STUDIES

The Foundation for Ancient Research and Mormon Studies (FARMS) encourages and supports research and publication about the Book of Mormon: Another Testament of Jesus Christ and other ancient scriptures.

FARMS is a nonprofit, tax-exempt educational foundation affiliated with Brigham Young University. Its main research interests in the scriptures include ancient history, language, literature, culture, geography, politics, religion, and law. Although research on such subjects is of secondary importance when compared with the spiritual and eternal messages of the scriptures, solid scholarly research can supply certain kinds of useful information, even if only tentatively, concerning many significant and interesting questions about the ancient backgrounds, origins, composition, and meanings of scripture.

The work of the Foundation rests on the premise that the Book of Mormon and other scriptures were written by prophets of God. Belief in this premise—in the divinity of scripture—is a matter of faith. Religious truths require divine witness to establish the faith of the believer. While scholarly research cannot replace that witness, such studies may reinforce and encourage individual testimonies by fostering understanding and appreciation of the scriptures. It is hoped that this information will help people to "come unto Christ" (Jacob 1:7) and to understand and take more seriously these ancient witnesses of the atonement of Jesus Christ, the Son of God.

The Foundation works to make interim and final reports about its research available widely, promptly, and economically, both in scholarly and in popular formats. FARMS publishes information about the Book of Mormon and other ancient scripture in the *Insights* newsletter, books and research papers, *FARMS Review of Books, Journal of Book of Mormon Studies,* reprints of published scholarly papers, and videos and audiotapes. FARMS also supports the preparation of the Collected Works of Hugh Nibley.

To facilitate the sharing of information, FARMS sponsors lectures, seminars, symposia, firesides, and radio and television broadcasts in which research findings are communicated to working scholars and to anyone interested in faithful, reliable information about the scriptures. Through Research Press, a publishing arm of the Foundation, FARMS publishes materials addressed primarily to working scholars.

For more information about the Foundation and its activities, contact the FARMS office at 1-800-327-6715 or (801) 373-5111. You can also visit the FARMS website at www.farmsresearch.com.